THE **LOST CIT**
IS KNOWN AROUNI

The Lost Cities Series:
Lost Cities of Atlantis, Ancient Europe and the Mediterranean
Lost Cities of Ancient Lemuria & the Pacific
Lost Cities of China, Central Asia & India
Lost Cities & Ancient Mysteries of Africa & Arabia
Lost Cities & Ancient Mysteries of South America
Lost Cities of North & Central America

The **Lost Cities of the Pacific Series**:
•ANCIENT TONGA & THE LOST CITY OF MU'A
•ANCIENT NEW ZEALAND & THE KAIMANAWA WALL
•ANCIENT MICRONESIA & THE LOST CITY OF NAN MADOL
•ANCIENT RAPA NUI & THE LOST LAND OF HIVA
•ANCIENT TAHITI & THE LOST CITY OF HAVAI'IKI

The **Lost Cities Series**:
•LOST CITIES OF ATLANTIS, ANCIENT EUROPE
 & THE MEDITERRANEAN
•LOST CITIES OF NORTH & CENTRAL AMERICA
•LOST CITIES & ANCIENT MYSTERIES OF SOUTH AMERICA
•LOST CITIES OF ANCIENT LEMURIA & THE PACIFIC
•LOST CITIES & ANCIENT MYSTERIES OF AFRICA & ARABIA
•LOST CITIES OF CHINA, CENTRAL ASIA & INDIA

The **Mystic Traveller Series**:
•IN SECRET TIBET by Theodore Illion (1937)
•DARKNESS OVER TIBET by Theodore Illion (1938)
•IN SECRET MONGOLIA by Henning Haslund (1934)
•MEN AND GODS IN MONGOLIA by Henning Haslund (1935)
•MYSTERY CITIES by Thomas Gann (1925)
•IN QUEST OF LOST WORLDS by Byron de Prorok (1937)

The **Atlantis Reprint Series**:
•ATLANTIS IN SPAIN by Elena Whishaw (1929)
•THE HISTORY OF ATLANTIS by Lewis Spence (1926)
•RIDDLE OF THE PACIFIC by John MacMillan Brown (1924)
•THE SHADOW OF ATLANTIS by Col. A. Braghine (1940)
•SECRET CITIES OF OLD SOUTH AMERICA by H. Wilkins (1952)

The **New Science Series**:
•THE FREE ENERGY DEVICE HANDBOOK
•THE FANTASTIC INVENTIONS OF NIKOLA TESLA
•THE ANTI-GRAVITY HANDBOOK
•ANTI-GRAVITY & THE WORLD GRID
•ANTI-GRAVITY & THE UNIFIED FIELD
•VIMANA AIRCRAFT OF ANCIENT INDIA & ATLANTIS

ANCIENT TONGA
& THE LOST CITY
OF MU'A

INCLUDING
SAMOA, FIJI,
& RAROTONGA

DAVID HATCHER CHILDRESS

THE LOST CITIES OF THE PACIFIC SERIES:

•ANCIENT TONGA & THE LOST CITY OF MU'A
Including Samoa, Fiji, and Rarotonga

•ANCIENT MICRONESIA & THE LOST CITY OF NAN MADOL
Including Ponape, Kosrae, Guam and Yap

•ANCIENT TAHITI & THE LOST CITY OF HAVAIIKI
Including the Marquesas & the Tuamotu Islands

•ANCIENT RAPA NUI & THE LOST LAND OF HIVA
Including Easter Island, Pitcairn, & the Austral Islands

•ANCIENT NEW ZEALAND & THE KAIMANAWA WALL
Including the Chatham Islands

ANCIENT TONGA & THE LOST CITY OF MU'A

ADVENTURES UNLIMITED PRESS

I dedicate this book to the "New Havai'iki."

"As above, so below." —Hermes Trismegistis

I would like to thank the many researchers who have helped me write this book, whether they know it or not. Thanks especially to T.H. Fale, Thor Heyerdahl, William Corliss, Tom Brown, Harry Osoff, and many others.

Ancient Tonga & the Lost City of Mu'A
©Copyright 1996
David Hatcher Childress

All rights reserved

Printed in the United States of America

First Printing

December 1996

ISBN 0-932813-36-4

Published by
Adventures Unlimited Press
Stelle, Illinois 60919 USA

Cover illustration of an ancient pyramid at Mu'A

TABLE OF CONTENTS

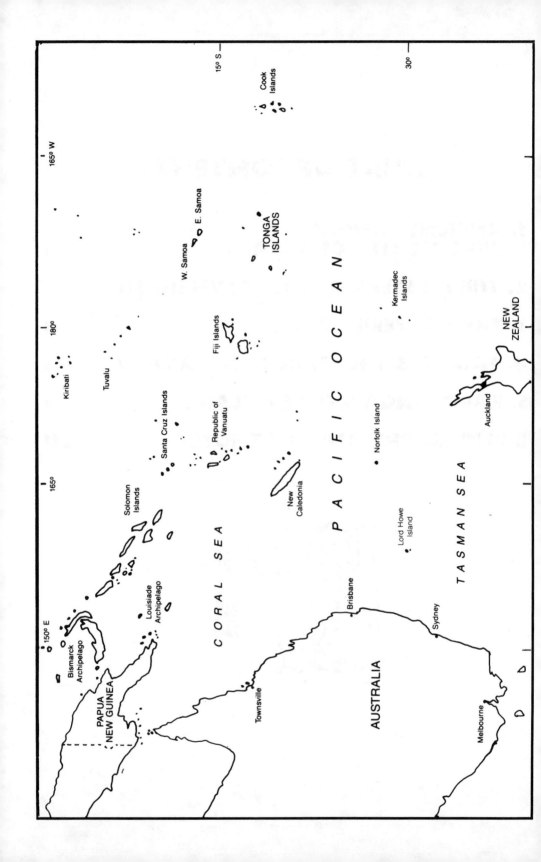

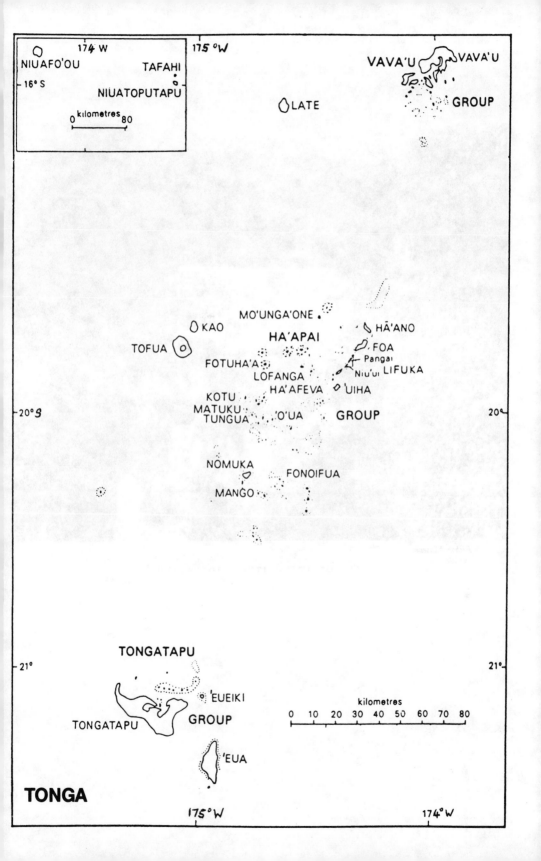

THE GREAT TRILITHON, TONGATABU

CHAPTER 1
ANCIENT TONGA:

THE LOST CITY OF MU'A

The canoe that came from Manuka
Was manned by a crew from the gods,
Maui-atalaga, Maui-motua,
Maui-kisikisi the wise...
He brought the wondrous hook,
He came and drew up lands...
—Tongan chant recorded by Peter S.
Buck

Tonga. Of all the islands in Polynesia Tonga is perhaps the most exotic. It shall be shown in this book that ancient Tonga stretched much farther into the Pacific than it does today. Indeed, one of the points of this book is that Tonga, at one time, was the capital of the entire Polynesia realm.

During the last half of the 19th century Pacific Island nations were being swallowed up by the colonial powers of Europe, Tonga alone had a sufficiently strong central government to retain their independence. Two centuries ago, the crowned heads of Europe recognized as fellow monarchs the kings of Hawaii, Fiji, Tahiti, Samoa, the Cook Islands and Tonga. Now all that is left of these ancient monarchies is the royal family of Tonga,

An old print of the pyramids of Tonga.

having ruled Tonga for the last 1,000 years. At the time of European domination of the world, only such countries with strong royal families as Thailand, Nepal, Japan and Ethiopia were able to retain independence and stay neutral in the power politics of the day. Tonga is the only Melanesian or Polynesian state never to be brought under colonial rule.

Why was Tonga, a small island kingdom, able to resist colonial occupation? The answer, I believe, is that Tonga had at one time been a very sophisticated capital of Polynesia, while in decline, still managed to retain more of its traditional government than other islands of the Pacific. While other islands had their kings and ruling families, all of these islands had at one point been ruled by the central government in Tonga. This central government was apparently set up thousands of years ago by the early Polynesian voyagers coming from Havaiiki. This mysterious land of Havaiiki has been discussed at great length by many authors, with various diverging conclusions being reached.

The search for Havaiiki, the homeland of Maui, is the search for the origins of the Polynesians. Does Havaiiki exist in the Pacific or somewhere else? Havaiiki has been placed in many locations: in Pacific islands such as Raiatea, Savaii, the Marquesas or Hawaii; and in Indonesia, the west coast of India or even Egypt. Others place Havaiiki in Mexico or Peru, or even in land which is now beneath the ocean, a land called Hiva by the natives of Rapa Nui/ Easter Island. The concept of sunken lands in the Pacific is a fascinating one, though one rarely considered by orthodox archaeologists.

Modern Tonga consists of about 150 islands, a number which changes from time to time because islands literally appear and disappear in the waters around Tonga. Only about 36 islands are populated, the other islands being too small or too infertile for human habitation. To the west of Tonga is Fiji, a large

An old print of the Tu'i Tonga.

island nation whose eastern-most islands, the Lau group, are quite close to the Ha'apai group of Tonga. Tonga ruled Fiji until a time just prior to the European expansion in the Pacific.

To the northeast of Tonga are the islands of Samoa and to the immediate east is the solitary island of Niue, today a self governing nation. To the southeast is Rarotonga in the Cook Islands. Tonga means "south" in most Polynesian dialects and Rarotonga mean "far-south." According to tradition, in ancient times Samoa, Niue and Rarotonga were ruled from Tonga, or specifically, Tongatapu.

An Island Archipelago

When Captain Cook visited the islands in 1773 he was impressed by the courtesy of the people, and nicknamed the group the "Friendly Islands," a name that has stuck to this day. Pyramids of food were given to Cook's crew in a lavish feast, along with displays of boxing prowess by the Tongans. Some say the islanders intended to roast Cook and his crew as part of a second feast, but the profuse thanks the Tongans received for their reception of Cook prompted the hosts to change their minds.

A scarlet broadcloth presented by Capt. Cook to the Tu'i Tonga, the paramount chief of the islands is still preserved on the main island. A male giant tortoise from the Galapagos Islands also given

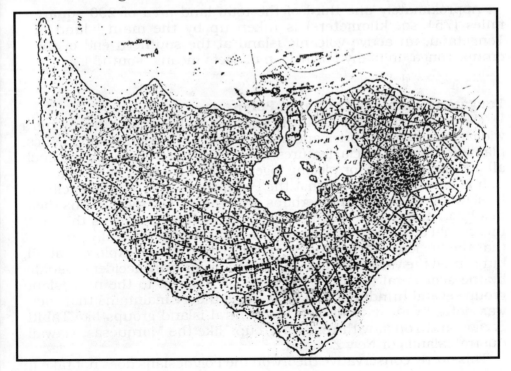

An old print of the ancient road system of Tonga.

to the islanders by Cook was allowed to wander blind in the queen's garden right up until 1966 when it died at the ripe old age of 200. Its mummified body can now be seen at the Tongan Cultural Center.

Cook found the islanders to be a friendly bunch, which might be thought of any islander who didn't attack and eat his guests. However, Tongans were in fact fierce warriors who frequently fought with the nearby Fiji Islanders aided by great double canoes. But in 1831, quite early in the Tongans' relationship with the Europeans, Wesleyan Methodist Christian missionaries converted the High Chief Taufa'ahau to Christianity. After uniting all of Tonga, he was crowned King George Tupou I, and in 1845 stopped the cannibal wars for good. Tonga became a British protectorate in 1900 and gained complete independence in 1970.

Tongans are literal giants. The present king of Tonga, Taufa'ahau Tupou IV is over six feet tall and weighs more than 300 pounds. He reserves two seats on any airline he flies. Tongans are perhaps a good example of why Polynesians are said to be the largest race of humans on our planet.

Approximately one third of the total land area of 290 square miles (751 sq. kilometers) is taken up by the main island of Tongatapu, an active volcanic island at the southern end of the group. Tonga, in many Polynesian dialects means "south."

Tongatapu: Ancient Capital of Polynesia

The settlement of the Pacific is a controversial subject that spans a wide spectrum of theories and a wide variety of evidence. Linguistics, plant distribution, racial features, stone building techniques and such all provide evidence for piecing together the history of Polynesia.

It is currently believed that the Polynesians entered the Pacific at least 3,500 years ago and perhaps even earlier. Overly cautious theories by archaeologists have often led to such proposals as the "drift theory" of Polynesian settlement. The "drift theory" basically proposes that the ancient Polynesians were not navigators or explorers at all, but settled the various islands of the Pacific by pure accident, usually by the accidental drifting of a canoe by a storm to the next island group several hundred miles away. This theory maintains that there was not a two-way trade between central island groups like Tahiti, Samoa and Tonga with remoter groups like the Marquesas, Hawaii, Austral Islands or New Zealand.

This overly conservative theory on the Polynesians does not take in regard the knowledge and science of the ancient Polynesians. As Peter S. Buck called them, they were truly the Vikings of the Sunrise, probably the greatest seafarers of the ancient world. Yet, unfortunately, the conservative theories denying deliberate Polynesian expansion throughout the Pacific has continued to affect the way we view ancient Polynesia.

Actually, the evidence suggests that Ancient Polynesia, with Tongatapu it's capital, was an extremely sophisticated nation which sailed the vast Pacific in huge ships, built gigantic pyramids, roads and monuments, and had great universities where navigation, astronomy, climatology and theological history were taught. This maritime empire existed for thousands of years and traded with powerful countries all around the Pacific rim, including North and South America. The people lived an idyllic existence for many hundreds of years until Polynesia fell into decline and a dark age swept through the Pacific.

The glory of the ancient Sun Empire of the Pacific, with it capital at Tongatapu, "Sacred Tonga," or "Sacred South," in Polynesian, can still be seen today its many ancient ruins, the trail in search of the mysteries of the Polynesia seems to naturally being in Tonga. There are many mysteries to consider: Who were the Polynesians and where

An old print of a pyramid done in 1797 by James Wilson for *A Missionary Voyage to the South Pacific Ocean.*

did they come from? Why did they build such huge monuments all over the Pacific? Was there a central government that controlled the Pacific and if so, where was it located? Did the Polynesians ever visit continental land masses such as the Americas, Australia and mainland Asia? Was Polynesia once part of a great trading empire that spanned the entire Pacific from India and China to the great civilizations of Peru and Mexico?

Lapita Pottery and Ancient Tonga

In the traditional view of ancient Tonga, the islands were first settled about 3,500 years ago as part of a movement of seafarers from the western islands of Indonesia to the Pacific Islands beyond New Guinea.

These early explorers, a Caucasian race, bypassed the already populated areas in Melanesia that included New Guinea, New Britain, New Ireland and the Solomon Islands. Archaeologists tell us that they eventually settled in Fiji, Tonga and Samoa, creating the first "Polynesian Kingdom."

New Zealand University of Canterbury archaeologist Ian Campbell says in his book *Island Kingdom: Tonga Ancient & Modern* that "items of material culture made and used by the earliest Polynesians were identical throughout the Samoa-Tonga-Fiji area, and collections of similar artifacts have been discovered in widely dispersed location in the islands of Melanesia. These include adzes made of both stone and clam shell with a distinctive oval-shaped cross-section, fishhooks of a particular design, oven-stones, and items of personal decoration. Most distinctive, however, is a style of pottery which archaeologists have called 'Lapita-ware' after the place in New Caledonia where it was first scientifically excavated and analyzed. Because of its distinctive styles, Lapita pottery is the most reliable guide to the distribution of the ancestors of the Polynesians. A variety of pots was made according to a very

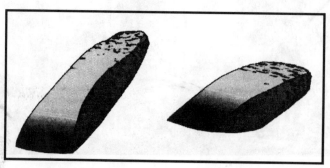

Adzes from the Lapita period.

stable convention as to shape; the pots were made without a potter's wheel but by being built up with small, flat slabs of clay, the joints being subsequently smoothed over; finally, this pottery was distinguished by its decoration, mostly patterns based on curved lines, often depicting a stylized human face, but often with straight lines or zig-zags as well, and drawn by pricking the soft clay with a pointed instrument."[3]

Of course, pottery making has been known for thousands of years and was in common use in India, China, and Pacific edge island groups like Sumatra, Java and Bali well over 3,500 years ago. Pottery virtually identical to that found on Tonga, Fiji and Samoa can be found at many sites in Melanesia as New Britain, Vanuatu and New Caledonia, where it was first discovered. On most Melanesian islands the pottery fragments are most commonly found on small islands or on northern or eastern sides of large islands like New Britain or New Caledonia. Says Campbell, "This pottery was the first in Melanesia, but the people who made it were not the first inhabitants of many of the places where it was found. This is consistent with the idea that the 'Lapita people' or 'ancestral Polynesians' were a new migration into the Pacific islands. Other evidence, however, especially linguistic, conflicts with this idea."[3]

Campbell is essentially saying that around 1500 B.C. a migration of Caucasian seafarers left from India or Indonesia and ventured eastward into the Pacific. The first islands that they discovered were already inhabited. They first passed either north or south of New Guinea, the largest island in the world (excluding Greenland), a mountainous, jungle-covered island that is populated by various highland and lowland tribes who, in ancient times (and arguably modern times as well) were in a continual state of warfare with each other. Anthropologists doubt that a central government ever ruled over New Guinea. The same goes for Australia, a continent populated by a similar race of people, however, the Trobriand Islands off the southeast coast of mainland New Guinea had a central government as did the Torres Straits Islanders of northern Queensland, Australia.

Other islands to the east were also inhabited by various

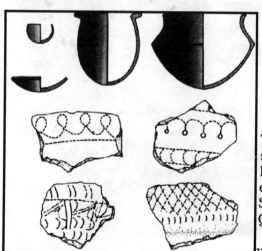

Pieces of Lapita pottery and pot shapes.

black races. The Solomon Islanders are said to have the darkest skin of any people and the origins of these people remains a mystery.

Incredibly, some archaeologists now claim that man has lived on various Melanesian Islands for at least 30,000 years! In an article in the prestigious journal *New Scientist* entitled "Pacific Islanders were the First Farmers," (*New Scientist*, Dec. 12, 1992, page 14) author Leigh Dayton points out that archaeologist J. Golson, formerly of the Australian National University, has found ditches and crude fields in New Guinea and other Melanesian Islands. The implication is that humans were tending plants here between 7,000 and 10,000 years ago.

The article further points out that on Buka Island in the Solomons, while excavating Kilu cave, archaeologists M. Spriggs and S. Wickler unearthed small flake tools with surfaces displaying starch grains and other plant residues. Evidently, these tools were used for processing taro. Further, the starch grains resembled those of cultivated rather than wild taro. The date for find was an astonishing 28,000 years before present! The article points out that a site at Wadi Kubbaniya, Egypt has been dated at 17,000 to 18,000 years old by G. Hillman of the Institute of Archaeology, London. This site also had grinding stones and tuber remains, but the Solomon Island discovery was 10,000 years older!

A similar site of human bones and tools was found in a semi-submerged cave on New Ireland and carbon-dating reveled an age of 30,000

An artist's impression of the Lapita site of Ha'ateiho, Tongatapu.

years B.P.

Similarly, New Caledonia has revealed some astonishing dates for ancient "concrete" structures found there. When some of the more than 400 gravel hills on New Caledonia were excavated in the 1960s, they had cement columns of lime and shell matter that was carbon dated by Yale and the New Caledonia Museum as having been made before 5120 B.C. and 10,950 B.C. These weird cement columns can be found in the southern part of New Caledonia and on the Isle of Pines.

A shard of Lapita pottery from Tonga.

Linguistically, the ancient Polynesians shared many similarities with Melanesia which suggest that both Polynesians and Melanesian shared the same ancestral language. Says Ian Campbell in *Island Kingdom,* "The affiliations for western Polynesia are strongest with that part of Melanesia which is closest, Vanuatu, implying that the earliest settlers of Tonga spoke the same language as many of the inhabitants of Vanuatu. This may imply that the Lapita people were or became integrated with the other inhabitants of Vanuatu, rather than remaining as fringe settlers on the margins of the islands preserving a distinctive culture. To complicate matters, all of the languages of Polynesia and Micronesia, together with many of the languages of Melanesia, can be traced through various stages, to a common ancestral language now called Austronesian which was probably spoken about 6,000 years ago."

It is a mystery as to how two different races and cultures such as Polynesians and Melanesians can have the same clearly identifiable root-language. One explanation, given by New Zealand professor Dr. Barry Fell, is that both languages arose from ancient Egyptian. Ancient Egypt was a seafaring nation that had both blacks and whites speaking the same language. Other linguists speculate that this language is proto-Malayan or proto-Aryan. Still, the mystery of the settlement of the Pacific and its many racial groups remains to be solved.

The Mystery of the Lapita People

The Lapita People continued out into the western Pacific, beyond the already inhabited Solomon Islands and the Vanuatu archipelago to the uninhabited islands of Fiji, Tonga and Samoa. Today Fiji is considered a Melanesian island but archaeologists also theorize that Fiji was originally a Polynesian island that was slowly invaded by Melanesians coming from the west. The eastern Lau Islands of Fiji were controlled by Tonga up to historical times.

The Lapita People existed for about a thousand years, say archaeologists, and then suddenly the use of pottery died out and the technology was lost. The pots became thinner and less hard due to lower kiln temperatures and the pots broke more easily and eventually their use was discontinued entirely.

From 1500 B.C. to 500 B.C. an empire of pottery making people spanned the western Pacific. It is this great pyramid that made the megaliths of Tonga, including the building of the city of Mu'a and Tonga's great Trilithon.

Ian Campbell describes the Lapita People, the progenitors of Tongan and Polynesian culture: "They had chiefs who were chosen by birth; they made tools from shell and stone for catching fish and digging the soil; they had nets for fishing and probably for catching birds as well; their hoses probably had rounded ends like modern Tongan houses; they had outrigger canoes and larger vessels made of two hulls. They knew the stars and the sea and winds well, and could navigate to distant islands beyond the horizon. They probably lived more from the sea than from the land, but they brought with them to Tonga the same food plants used elsewhere in the Pacific—the coconut, talo (known as taro elsewhere), breadfruit, yam and banana. They also brought the rat, the pig, the dog and the fowl."[3]

These amazing people, probably the world's greatest seafarers, remain largely a mystery to us, but their great monuments remain. Writers like Campbell are mystified by the sudden decline in civilization and see these people as isolated from each other and

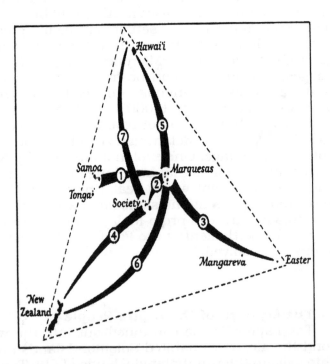

One theory on the order of primary migrations of the Polynesians, starting in Tonga & Samoa (after Emory and Sinoto).

other island archipelagos. Says Campbell, "...it seems probable that the people who lived in Tonga became isolated from each other, and from people in the nearby island groups." Campbell says that evidence for this hypothesis is the differences in cultures between Fiji, Tonga, Samoa and other island areas. Later, near to the time of European contact, island travel between Fiji, Tonga and Samoa resumed and the Tongans imported clay pots from Fiji.

Polynesia went through many dark ages, but it is more likely that the Tongans never lost the ability to make long ocean journeys. In fact, evidence indicates that Tonga was the central naval base for a pan-Pacific empire that existed for thousands of years and had only fallen into decline a few hundred years before European contact.

However, circa 500 B.C. the larger Empire of the Pacific, with Tongatapu its capital, collapsed and the western islands such as New Caledonia and Fiji were inaccessible to Tonga and Samoa. A constant state of warfare existed between the Melanesians and the Polynesians, and the front line in this war was Fiji. Fiji was ultimately lost, and Tonga withdrew from mainland Fiji.

Evidence indicates that the large Tongan double canoes were still in use between Fiji, Samoa and Tonga up to the time of European contact. There is no reason to suspect that this ever stopped throughout the history of Polynesia. Rather, it was the long voyages between Eastern Polynesia and Western Polynesia that were that were increasingly rare. Remote areas of the Polynesian Triangle such as Hawaii, Rapa Nui and New Zealand had lost contact with the rest of Polynesia around 1300 A.D. Before this time, long ocean voyages still took place, notably the voyage of the Warrior Maoris from the Marquesas to invade New Zealand circa 1250 A.D.

Tonga and the whole of Polynesia were definitely in the decline when European ships began to explore the Pacific. But when was the megalithic period of Tonga and the Pacific and who were these people. Traditional archaeologists have maintained that the langi pyramids and trilithon of Tonga were built quite recently, while other archaeologists, including myself, believe that these megaliths are from the earlier period of the Lapita People.

The God-Kings of Tonga

The known history of Tonga begins with the legends of the God-Kings of Tonga. Legends concerning the origin of the Tu'i Tonga, or king of Tonga, say that the god Tangaloa came to earth and became the father of a boy named 'Aho'eitu. The god Tangaloa fell in love with a Tongan women who was to bear his son, but left Tonga before the son was born. Tongaloa returned to his home in the sky and the boy was brought up by his mother.

One day 'Aho'eitu asked his mother about his father, and she told him where he could find his father. The boy traveled to where the gods lived, and was welcomed by Tangaloa who was glad to see his son. 'Aho'eitu also discovered, however, that he had four half-brothers by his father who were older than him. These half-brothers were jealous of him and plotted to kill him.

The four half-brothers killed 'Aho'eitu, chopped his head off and the rest of him into pieces. They threw his head into the bushes and ate the rest of him. Tangaloa was angry when he discovered this crime against his son and made the half-brothers vomit what they eaten into a bowl. 'Aho'eitu was thus reconstituted and restored to life. The half-brothers were compelled to honor and re-

A Tongan double canoe in its shed at Vavau. Drawn in 1839 by Dumont-d'Urville's artist, L. le Breton (courtesy of the Turnbull Library, Wellington). Note the huge size of the vessel, easily capable of transoceanic voyages.

spect 'Aho'eitu as their superior and serve him as their lord, even though he was younger than them.

'Aho'eitu was then sent back to Tonga to rule as the Tu'i Tonga, representing his divine father. His half-brothers who had tried to remove him were forced by their father to serve 'Aho'eitu in perpetuity. 'Aho'eitu became the first king of Tonga and all the subsequent kings of Tonga, the Tu'i Tongas, are reputedly descended from him. 'Aho'eitu was the paramount ruler of all the land that Tongatapu controlled and was the earthly representative of the divine. He was a god-king who ancestry was directly traced to the gods themselves.

God-kings are fairly common in the ancient world and a few, including the present king of Tonga, still survive today. God-kings were common in ancient Egypt, ancient India, ancient Japan, the Meso-America, Tibet, and other areas of the world. Current God-Kings who continue to rule, in one fashion or another, are the Emperor of Japan, the King of Nepal (who is an incarnation of the Hindu god Vishnu), the king of Thailand, and the royal family of Tonga.

Today, genealogists are only able to trace the Tu'i Tonga line of kingship back through 39 title-holders. According to the genealogies of Tongan royalty, the Tu'i Tonga title was passed down from father to favorite son and the last person have the actual title of Tuitonga was Laufilitonga, great-grandfather of the current king. Laufilitonga passed away on in 1865 and was ostensibly the thirty-ninth person in his dynasty to carry the title.

Archaeologists like Campbell assume that the average reign for a Tu'i Tonga was 25 years, then the 39 holders would amount to a

A portion of one of the stepped langi at Lapaha.

period of 975 years. This then places the beginning of the current dynastic succession as beginning in 875 A.D. This is only an approximate date, and the list of kings is admitted to contain errors, as there are several different versions still extant. While it has often been assumed that 'Aho'eitu, as the first of these god-kings, would have existed at about this period, the late ninth century A.D. However, there is evidence that the dynasty of the Tu'i Tongas goes back much further than 875 A.D.

The lists of the names of the Tu'i Tonga is known to contain certain errors, and when it comes to the oldest names, they be the names of family dynasties lasting for hundreds of years, rather than the names of individuals, as the list would have grown impossibly long to memorize.

According to Ian Campbell, "For several hundred years, all that is known of the Tongan kings is what is told in legends and genealogies passed down from generation to generation over the centuries. Although this information was taught very exactly to ensure its correct transmission, there were nevertheless different versions of genealogies and legends which show that errors did creep in. For this reason the reconstruction of much Tongan history before the period of written records is tentative."

Like other Polynesian myths, and myths around the world, the deeds of the early kings are lost in the legends of time. No actual tales have survived of the first nine kings in the Tu'i Tonga line. The first Tu'i Tonga about whom any detailed stories are known is the Tenth Tu'i Tonga, Momo. The story of Momo concerns his advisor Lo'au, a man who made great voyages and introduced many changes and new ideas to Tonga.

About Momo and Lo'au Campbell says, "The Tongan historian, Futa Helu, has argued that Lo'au was a Samoan, or at least a foreigner, perhaps even from Eastern Polynesia and who became an influential man because of his great wisdom and ability. He is said to have conducted great voyages, to have made major changes in the organization of Tonga,

A completely quarried slab waiting to be lifted out of Pangaimotu Quarry. A fragment of a broken slab is at the right.

and to have introduced foreign ideas."[3]

Lo'au is an important figure in Tongan "mythology" because he is credited with many innovations to Tongan society including the introduction of kava (Indian pepper-root), and the ceremonies that went with drinking it. Kava ceremonies reinforced the social system by declaring the ranks of the various chiefs, and reminded everyone of the absolute superiority of Tu'i Tonga.

Ancient Tonga had a caste system divided into three parts: The first was the aristocracy Hou'eiki, which included the Tu'i Tonga himself. Second was the Mu'a, the chiefs of Tonga and its various island domains. The third was the Tu'a or common people.

This period of Tonga, sometimes known as the "classic" phase was a time of a Tongan Empire, when great ships sailed from the city of Mu'a and the lagoon of Tongatapu to the many corners of the Polynesian world and beyond. One can imagine hundreds of the large double-canoes, each holding 300 to 400 people, lying at anchor in the protected harbor that - is Tongatapu's main feature. "These political changes might also be connected with the story that Lo'au suppressed cannibalism in Tonga... The stories of Lo'au's voyaging may

A partially quarried slab at Pangaimotu Quarry. It was initially planned to have been larger and was then reduced in size, but still never completed.

Ancient Tonga   25

James Churchward's 1876 drawing of the Ha'amonga Trilithon.

also indicate a growing propensity of Tongans of that time to travel; it was after this time that Tongan influence became felt in distant islands, and some legends speak of a Tongan empire." Campbell states.

But when was this great empire? If it was 39 kings of Tonga ago, that would make this golden age of Tonga at about 875 A.D. Yet, this "classical age" of Tonga would seem to have occurred before this time, more like about 1000 B.C. Was the time of the early kings actually a time coinciding with the early Lapita People?

The Ha'amonga of Maui

The Ha'amonga a Maui trilithon, or "Burden of Maui," is a gigantic stone archway fifteen feet high and eighteen feet long. Walking around it, one can marvel at the feat of engineering that has created this impressive monument.

It consists of an arch made from two upright pillars each 4.88 meters high (approximately. 15 feet), each weighing approximately 50 tons and supporting a central lintel which is 5.79 meters long (approximately. 18 feet) and weighs an estimated 8,165 kilograms (8.165 metric tons or approximately 18,000 pounds or 9 American tons). The top stone was set into grooves

T.H. Fale's traditional mat design that he says is based on the astronomy of the Ha'amonga Trilithon.

carved into the upright stones, rather than having merely been set on top as had been done at Stone Henge. Walking around it I noticed grooves in the stones, possibly from utilization of the arch as an instrument for determining the seasons. It seemed to have much the same purpose as Stone Henge in England.

Indeed, on June 21, 1967, the present king had observed the sunrise from this spot, which accurately corresponded to a line drawn on the lintel.

The origins of the massive monument are controversial. One tradition in Tonga says that Ha'amonga a Maui was built by Tu'itatui, the eleventh Tu'i Tonga by the mythological ancestor count. Tu'itatui was the son of Momo and Nua, the daughter of the enterprising advisor Lo'au. Mythologically it is said that Tu'itatui was the builder of the arch and the large standing stone to the east of the arch.

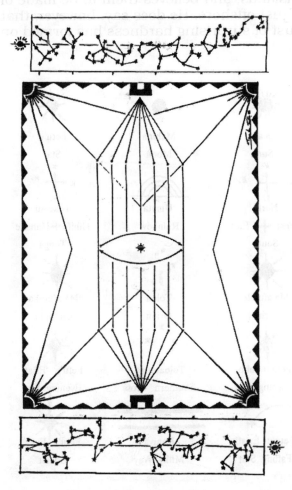

The story is told that this son of Momo and Nua would stand with his back to the large stone slab, called the Maka Fakinanga, and swing a stout stick at knee level when addressing his chiefs. The swinging stick was to keep his advisors and chiefs from getting too close to him and the stone slab protected his back.

While many archeologists have assumed from genealogies that Tu'itatui lived circa 1200, or 250 years after the assumed 39 kings point. However, if the arch was built at this period, the people seem to have lost all memory of its purpose. It is quite likely that this important monument was built at about the same time as the arrival of the Lapita People, about 1500 B.C.

In an article in the

T.H. Fale's star chart based on the Ha'amonga Trilithon.

Royal Anthropological Institute Journal in 1902 (Number 32, pages 81-88), British Anthropologist Basil Thomason says that common tradition has it that the arch was erected by the god Maui with stones that he brought from Uvea (Wallis Island) in a giant canoe. Thomason says that this is tantamount to the islanders professing ignorance as to their origin, as Maui is given the credit for everything that cannot be explained. "It is further alleged that in the reef at Uvea the holes from which these stones had been quarried may still be seen, and that the stone is of a kind not found in Tonga." He then goes on to say that a Tongan chief was quoted in the 1799 book, *Voyage of the Duff* as having stated that the stones had been brought in a double canoe from the island of Lefooga (Lifuka) in the Haapai group.[25]

Thomason discounts the legend which states that the stones were brought from other islands, and believes them to be made of coral quarried on the reef just offshore. He does say, however, that he believes that a lime crust of surprising hardness has formed on the outside of the stones.

"Their purpose will always remain a matter of conjecture," he says. "At first sight they suggest a gateway to some sacred spot inland, but I have examined the bush for some distance in their neighborhood, and have found no trace of ruins, or stones of any kind. Moreover, the memory of sacred spots dies very hard in Tonga, and the natives do not believe them to have been a gateway. I have lately received from Mateialona, the Governor of Haapai and cousin to the king, a letter in answer to one of mine on this subject. He

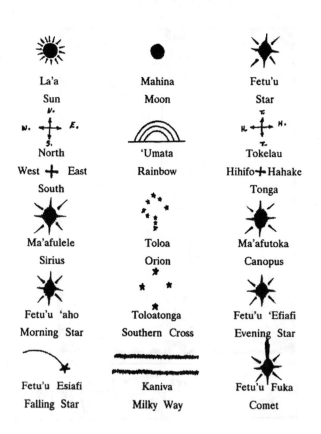

T.H. Fale's list of Tongan astronomical symbols.

La'a — Sun

Mahina — Moon

Fetu'u — Star

North / West — East / South

'Umata — Rainbow

Tokelau

Hihifo — Hahake / Tonga

Ma'afulele — Sirius

Toloa — Orion

Ma'afutoka — Canopus

Fetu'u 'aho — Morning Star

Toloatonga — Southern Cross

Fetu'u 'Efiafi — Evening Star

Fetu'u Esiafi — Falling Star

Kaniva — Milky Way

Fetu'u Fuka — Comet

says: 'Concerning the Haamonga of Maui, they say forsooth that a Tui Tonga (the sacred line of chiefs), named Tui-ta-tui, erected it, and that he was so named because it was a time of assassination. And they say that he had it built for him to sit upon during the Faikava (ceremony of brewing kava), when the people sat around him in a circle, and that the king so dreaded assassination that he had this lordly seat built for himself that he might sit out of reach of his people. And this, they say, is the origin of the present custom of the Faikava, it being now forbidden for anyone to sit behind the king.'"[25]

At this juncture in his article, Thomason then makes a very interesting point: "But though the Haamonga monument is thus assigned by native tradition to the fourteenth century, there are considerations which point to the later date (sometime before the ascribed time of Tui-ta-tui, as in the legend of the god Maui bringing the stones from another island). For the quarrying and mortising of stones weighing some 50 tons apiece the craft of stonecutting must have been fully developed."[25] Thomason then goes on to explain how other monuments ascribed to a later period in the history of Tonga are much smaller and of much cruder workman-

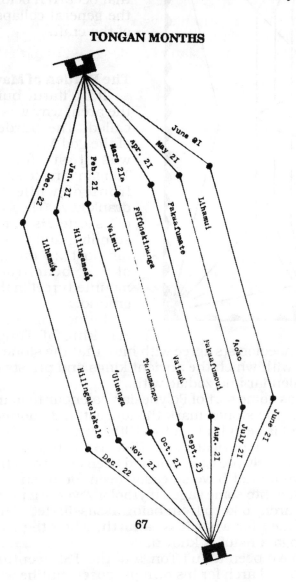

TONGAN MONTHS

67

T.H. Fale's calculation of the astronomy of the Ha'amonga Trilithon.

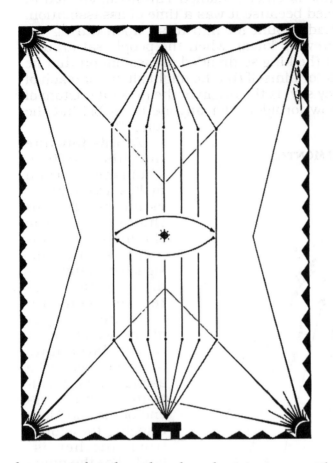

T.H. Fale's traditional mat design based on Tongan astronomy .

ship. He then concludes that the same stone-cutters could not have made both, and that the arch must be much older, from a time of stone-working excellence that occurred before the general collapse of the craft.

The Burden of Maui

If Tu'itatui built the arch, why was it called "The burden of the god Maui" if it was just for a Tongan king to sit in front of while he drank kava. The slab of stone is still standing and it is a nine foot (2.7 m) slab of beachrock mounted erect in the ground.

Rather, the modern king of Tonga has postulated, and archaeologists agree with him, that the stone is an astronomical device with which the ancient kings and priests of Tonga measured the calendar and zodiac with.

At the very least it was some sort of Polynesian calendar to mark the seasons. Notches on the stones mark the longest and shortest days of the year, but had it been built in the 13th century? Or had it been erected by the great navigators of 1500 B.C., the Lapita People? The later is most likely the case. If it had been erected in the 13th century, its use would not have so easily been forgotten and the entire structure falling into some vague mythology where a paranoid king has built the arch to keep from being assassinated. This story of Tu'itaui is revealed for what it is, a myth, when the true purpose of the Ha'amonga a Maui is known.

Tu'itatui may well have been a Tu'i Tonga of the 13th century who used the stone slab and arch for his own purposes, but he was probably not the builder of the monuments. They had stood there for many hundreds of years before him, when the Lapita People had arrived in Tonga.

The name Tu'itatui is a reiteration of the king's title, and has the mark of a mythological character who may be an amalgamation of an entire dynasty circa 1000 B.C. Three Tu'i Tongas were assassinated in the late 14th and 15th centuries, Havea I while bathing in the sea, his great-grandson, Havea II, by his Fijian retainer whom he trusted, and the son of Havea II, Takalaua. Takalaua was murdered by a conspiracy of chiefs who deemed him a tyrant after forcing the people to work for him during yam-planting seasons. The role of the Tu'i Tonga was a hazardous one and assassination stories feature strongly into the myths of Tonga.

It may well be that an accurate genealogical accounting of historically factual kings may not begin until the beginning king's current dynasty. This dynasty is known as the third dynasty and it

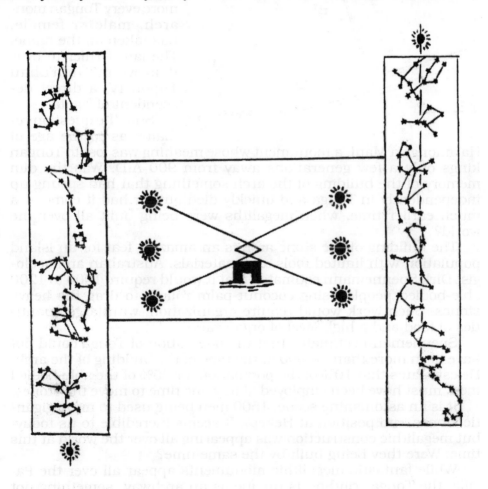

T.H. Fale's star chart from of the Ha'amonga Trilithon.

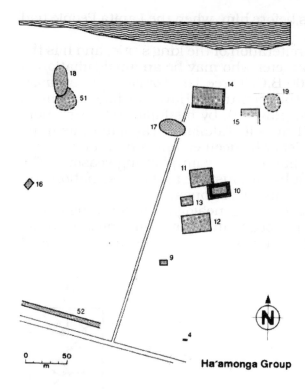

Ha'amonga Group

began around the year 1600 with a new Samoan dynasty in Tonga. The first king of this last dynasty was called Ngata Tu'i Kanokupolu, after Upolu, Samoa's second largest island and most fertile. Ngata, as he was known, began the practice of adding the name Tupou to their own name. This became a regular habit and for the past two centuries or more every Tongan monarch, male or female, has taken on the name. The latest ruler to bear it is King Taufa'ahau Tupou IV, a direct descendent of Ngata.

Still, the question remains as to the age of Ha'amonga a Maui, a monument whose meaning was lost to Tongan kings only a few generations away from 900 A.D. Was the dim memory of the building of the arch something that had sprung up independently in Tonga and quickly died out, or had it come at a much earlier time, when megaliths were being built all over the world?

The building of the stone arch is an amazing feat for an island population with limited tools and materials. Australian archaeologist Dirk Spennemann estimated that it would require 1000 to 1200 able-bodied people using coconut-palm rollers to drag the heavy stones. Such work would require organization, with large quantities of food and a high level of organization.

Spennemann estimates that the population of Tonga could not have been more than 16,000 at the time of the building of the arch. He estimates that 10% of the population, or 25% of the able-bodied men, must have been employed at any one time to move the stones.

It is an astonishing scene, 1500 men being used to move gigantic stones into position at Heketa. It seems incredible to us today, but megalithic construction was appearing all over the world at this time. Were they being built by the same time?

While fantastic megalithic monuments appear all over the Pacific, the Tonga trilithon is unique as an archway, something not

The Ha'amonga Trilithon, The Burden of Maui.

usually seen on Pacific Islands. The fact that the only megalithic arch in the Polynesia is found at Tongatapu is direct evidence that Tonga was once the capital of all the Pacific, with classes in astronomy being conducted at the Ha'amonga a Maui.

Polynesia's Astronomical College

Tonga was apparently once the center of the Polynesian astronomical elite, and it seems likely that navigators, especially the sons of the island chiefs all over the Pacific, were sent to Tonga to study the sacred knowledge of the sky.

A number of modern Tongan scholars now believe this, including Tavita H. Fale, the author of the books *Tongan Astronomy*[34] and *Through Polynesian Eyes*.[35] Fale demonstrates in his books that the Tongans, and Polynesians in general, had an excellent knowledge of astronomy and celestial navigation in the ancient past. Fale maintains that the Tongan's had names for every constellation in the sky and that the Ha'amonga Trilithon was part of the ancient Tongan observatory, the high priests of an ancient Polynesian "Sun Cult" or "Star Cult".

Fale did experiments while attending college in the United States to prove to himself that the markings on top of the Ha'amonga Trilithon could be used as a sophisticated astronomical device. His

results are detailed in his two books.

Fale demonstrates that the ancient Polynesians could navigate by the stars, did not need a compass, and that they generally knew where they were going. Certainly there must have been early journeys of exploration, but generally the Polynesian navigator knew which island he was heading for and which star would guide him to the island he sought. Even distant lands like Peru, Mexico or China could be reached by following certain stars.

Tonga with its astronomical observatory and sheltered lagoon for the great canoes made Tonga the ideal naval base for commanding the entire Pacific. From Tonga the great ships went in every direction. They made the early voyages to eastern Polynesia, establishing an eastern capital on the island of Raiatea in the Tahitian Islands.

Ships from Hawaii and Kiribati made the long journeys south to Samoa, Tonga or Tahiti. Southern Islands such as Rapa Nui, Rapa Iti and Rarotonga were also in contact with the ships. New Zealand was probably also visited by early seafarers from Tonga hundreds of years before the Warrior Maoris invaded from the Marquesas. It was a far-flung ocean empire that involved many islands and many ships. By the time of the European exploration in the Pacific only Tonga and Samoa still had the large ocean going canoes capable of the long voyages.

The Ancient Sun Cult of the Pacific

If the Ha'amonga a Maui was built thousands of years ago, as were the pyramids at Mu'a, does this shed more light on the Lapita People? Clearly, the Lapita People, the ancient Polynesians, were a highly sophisticated people who not only built large boats but knew how to navigate by using the stars, currents, waves and seasonal winds. Not only this, but they were expert stone-cutters who not only built with gigantic blocks of stone but fitted them expertly together when the structure required such precision.

It is not the scope of this book to talk in detail of the megalithic ruins all over the Pacific, but suffice it to say that structures and statues on Rapa Nui, Tahiti, the Marquesas and Tonga are lasting testimony to the genius of these people. Amazing structures such as Nan Madol on Pohnpei Island in Micronesia may have been originally been built by the early Polynesians, even though the island is occupied today by Micronesians of a Philipino origin. The remote north-western atoll of Kapingamaringi is a Polynesian island that is close to Pohnpei. Because the Kapingamaringi Atoll had a serious water shortage about 20 years ago most of the islanders, all Polynesian, were removed to Pohnpei where they created their own Polynesian village on the Micronesian island.

In order to solve the riddle of the Lapita People, we have think about the kind of people who typically build massive stone arches and terraced pyramids. Stonehenge comes to mind, but the when, why, who and how of that monument is as much a mystery as is the Tongan Trilithon. Yet, it is in Europe and the Mediterranean area that most stone arches can be found. We now come back to the origin of Polynesian people. If Polynesians are descendants of Libyan sailors, as Dr. Fell asserts, then we have an arch-building, megalith-constructing, sea-going culture that is not only capable of building such an edifice, but also is interested in the seasons.

Could it be that the Ha'amonga of Maui is actually several thousand years old? This would explain the ignorance of locals as to its origin. It would only be natural that local chiefs would hold important ceremonies around it. The legend of Tui-ta-tui seems to come from the fact that he was afraid of assassination, but he sat with his back to the single upright stone, yet he apparently had no knowledge of the ancient stone's actual purpose. Its purpose was as a sighting stone for the arch itself.

A highly organized group of scientist-priests would be needed to keep the knowledge alive. A center for learning would have to be created for students to learn navigation, astronomy and the ancient customs of the homeland. A society that spanned the entire Polynesian world like a religious cult, a cult of the sun and stars. This special university island was Tongatapu.

In an article in *American Anthropologist,* volume 17, published in 1915, the author, W. H. R. Rivers, discusses what he calls a "sun-cult" that existed throughout the Pacific. He believed that the Tonga Arch was part of this ancient

Will Mariner in Tonga.

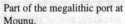

Part of the megalithic port at Mounu.

"secret society". Says Rivers: "The island of the Pacific which holds examples of megalithic structures most closely resembling those of other parts of the world is Tongatapu, where there are trilithic monuments so like those of Europe that the idea of a common source must rise to the mind of even the most strenuous advocate of independent origin. It is not possible at present to bring these monuments into relation with those of other parts of Oceania by connecting them with a cult of the sun, but Hambruch tells us that tradition points to the builders of the stonework of Ponape (Pohnpei) having come from Tonga. It may be that Tongatapu forms the intermediate link between the stonework of the Carolines and the megalithic monuments of other parts of the world."[25,83]

The article goes on to say that the idea of an ancient civilization worshipped the sun while building megalithic monuments is closer to the truth than probably any other theory. The remnant of such a civilization would be what formed Polynesian civilization as it had been found by the first European explorers in the 16th and 17th

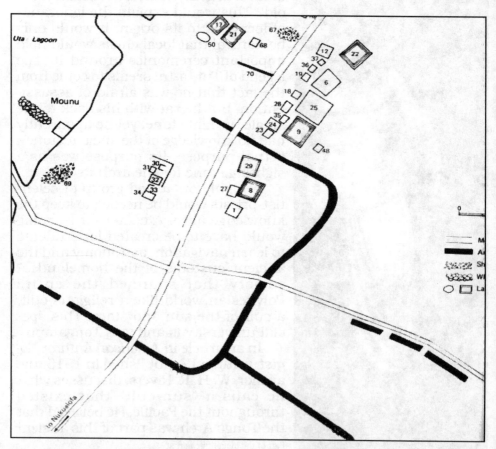

Map of the pyramids of Mu'a and the megalithic port of Mounu. The moat appears as a dark black line.

centuries. On Raiatea in the Tahiti group Captain Cook picked up a priest navigator who drew a map of Polynesia for Cook. The map contained Tonga, Samoa, Tahiti and many other islands, but did not include Hawaii, Rapa Nui or New Zealand, indicating the knowledge had fallen into decline. The great navigators had ceased their long voyages.

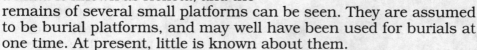

The area around the Ha'amonga a Maui is known as Heketa, and the remains of several small platforms can be seen. They are assumed to be burial platforms, and may well have been used for burials at one time. At present, little is known about them.

Tongan oral tradition implies that the first capital of Tonga was at Toloa, an area somewhere near the current Fua'amotu International Airport. Its precise location is not known but small mounds are known to exist in this area. Toloa seems to have vanished.

Oral tradition says the capital was moved to Heketa by the tenth Tu'i Tonga, Momo. The capital was said to exist among the platforms that can be seen between the Ha'amonga a Maui and the nearby sea. The coast is very rough in this area of the coast and it is a difficult place to land a large canoe. It is therefore a terrible spot for a capital city and there is some doubt that it was ever intended to be a capital city at all. The ancient canal city of Mu'a was probably already functioning in this capacity.

The Langi of Mu'a

The building of the ancient capital city of Mu'a must have begun many thousands of years ago when the island was slightly lower in relation to ocean and the lagoon. Tonga has risen about a meter over the last few thousand years and such constructions as the wharf at Mounu (Mu'nu) or the canal/moat are now useless. This is quite possibly the reason for the abandonment of Mu'a, the fact that the water in the lagoon was lower.

With its sheltered lagoon as an ideal harbor for a huge fleet of ships, a capital city with a large stone wharf and canals would only be natural. This early capital was clearly Mu'a. While the small area of Heketa by the Ha'amonga a Maui is said to have been the early capital, it was probably the isolated religious district where navigation and astronomy were taught. It existed at the same time as Mu'a and it was at Heketa that the priests resided. They monitored daily the rising and setting of the sun and at night the movements

Spiral design engraved in rock near Kawhia in Northwest New Zealand.

of the stars.

The Langi Tauhala, a pyramidical platform at the old fortress of Tongatapu is a cut stone block massive in size and is similar to the stones at Baalbek, Lebanon, the largest cut stones in the world, weighing an estimated 2,000 (two thousand) tons apiece. The largest stone at Langi Tauhala is 7.4 meters in length and 2.2 meters in height; it has a thickness of .4 meters and weighs an estimated 30 or 40 metric tons. It is part of a wall that is 222 meters long, and had been built at a time of great antiquity.

It is also interesting to note that the largest block is notched, and that the next block, cut to fit into this notch. Such construction indicates that the builders were aware of earthquakes and general cataclysmic shifts of the earth. "Keystone" cuts and such are ways of binding walls together, and had been done at Tiahuanaco and Ollantaytambo in South America. These stones are so massive, it is hard to imagine them going anywhere. Why should they be notched if not in anticipation of earth changes?

In fact, this massive block now has a crack that was probably caused by an earthquake. The wall that it is a part of must have been a part of a much larger structure at one time, yet, today, it is difficult to see just what function this long wall would have served. It is not part of any "tomb" or other large structure. The curved notching of this large stone is a sign that the stone masons that worked on the Tongan megaliths were quite sophisticated in their construction techniques. This knowledge of advanced stone masonry is unlikely to have developed independently in Tonga and probably came from the original homeland of the Polynesians. This homeland would have been a land where megalithic architecture and fine stone masonry were well known. Such a land could have been ancient India, Egypt, the Middle East or South America, all places with megalithic architecture.

The Canals and Docks of Mu'a

The central area of Mu'a was surrounded by a huge canal, or moat. This gigantic canal is so large, it was thought to be a "sunken road" to early archaeologists, who could not believe that giant canal fortifications where built, or needed, by the early Tongans.

Furthermore, the massive rocks at the ancient port on the lagoon side of Mu'a are evidence of the docking of huge transoceanic vessels in ancient times. The port at Mu'a was already an ancient ruin, unused by the Tongans, at the time of European colonization of the Pacific.

Dirk Spennemann in *Pathways to the Tongan Past*,[48] says "Mu'a offers a sheltered berthing place for canoes. It is located on the eastern shore of Fanga'uta lagoon, reasonably near the entrance, protected from the adverse seas by the Nukuleka peninsula. Like Heketa, the newly founded capital of Mu'a, with its Lapaha and Tatakamotonga districts, was a planned capital. But unlike Heketa, Mu'a seems to have started as a formidable fortification, the first known for Tonga. The still visible ditches are about 10-12 m deep (undoubtedly much deeper when first dug). The fortification was quadrangular, with one side open to the lagoon where canoes could be berthed or pulled ashore into canoe houses. The fortification suggests that the move Heketa represented both the fear of possible internal struggles and of outside attack."

Indeed, as Spennemann suggests, the early fortifications at Mu'a were an immense undertaking! A large canal originally came from the lagoon and surrounded several of the large pyramids, though

Part of the ancient wharf at Mounu, now overgrown.

the largest remained outside the moat area and were probably built later. "It is not yet known which is the oldest tomb, although it is likely that the first was erected inside the fortification."[48] states Spennemann

Spennemann, like most archaeologists, calls the monumental pyramids "tombs" though this writer maintains that they were not originally built as tombs, but as fortified ceremonial structures. During warfare, the Tongan army could withdraw to the safety of the pyramids that were surrounded by the moat/canal.

There are some indications that the canal at Mu'a extended further into the interior of the island. One of the canals extends from the northwest corner of Mu'a and extends into the interior while portions of another canal have been discovered extending west toward the village of Haveluliku, running parallel with the modern road. It is interesting to speculate whether or not these ancient canals were part of a sophisticated system that once reached into the interior of the island, allowing ships to enter from the ocean into the large lagoon and then either dock at the wharf at Mounu or move further into the island using the canals.

The emerging picture of ancient Tonga is one of an extremely advanced culture that built a sophisticated system of roads, canals, monumental pyramids, and other large stone remains. The entire island was probably densely populated, much as it is today. Roads left Mu'a in all directions, and the large double canoes and reed ships could even enter into the interior of the island by utilizing the canals. The glory of ancient Tonga has almost been forgotten, but the monumental ruins of this ancient land continue to signal the present day with a hint of the former greatness when Tonga was the capital of Polynesia.

Hawaiian spiral design engraved in rock.

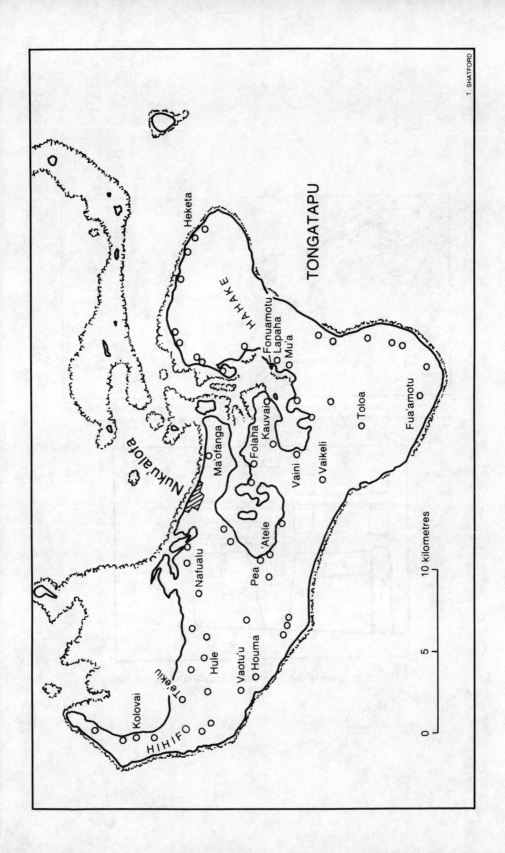

TONGATAPU

HAHAKE

Heketa

Fonuamotu
Lapaha
Mu'a

Toloa

Fua'amotu

Vaikeli

Vaini

Kauvai

Folaha

Ma'ofanga

Nuku'alofa

'Atele

Nafualu

Pea

Vaotu'u
Houma

Hule

O'Teleku

Kolovai

HIHIFO

0   5   10 kilometres

T. SHATFORD

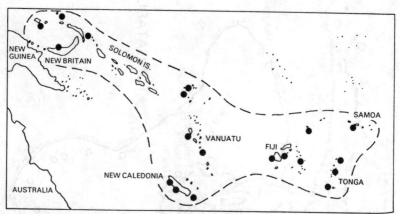

Sites containing Lapita pottery, indicated by black dots on this map of the southwestern Pacific, are distributed from the area of New Britain, through island Melanesia, and as far east as Samoa and Tonga.

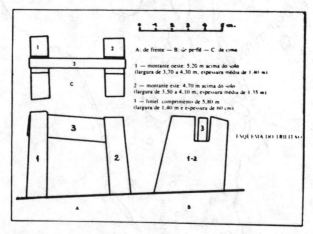

A French diagram of the Ha'amonga Trilithon's construction.

One of the Langi at Lapaha. Note the finely cut stones and the fact that the pyramid-platforms were at one time completely overgrown by trees, roots and bushes. A considerable clearing of the langi has taken place for this photo indicating that the langi were not being used for hundreds of years.

The ancient langi Tauhala at Mu'a. Probably the largest block of stone used in construction of the pyramids at Mu'a, it is curiously notched into the block on its right. This huge slab of beachrock has been split by an earthquake since this photo was taken, circa 1900.

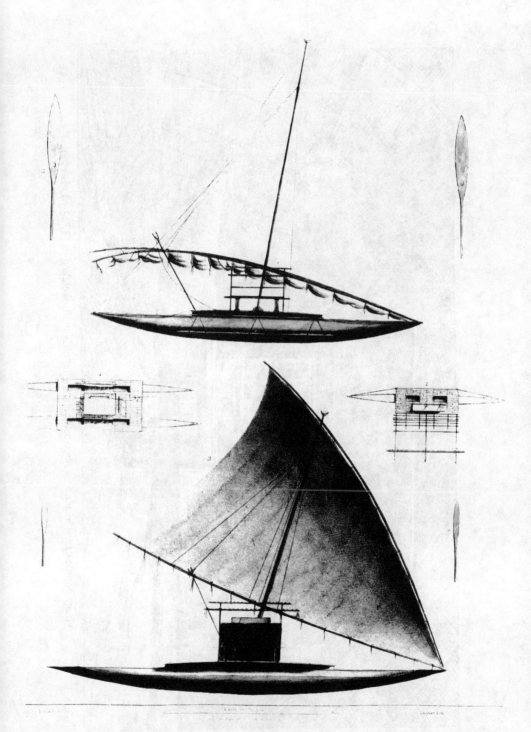

Plan of a canoe recorded in Tonga during the voyage of *L'Astrolab*, 1826–29 (D'Urville 1833).

A huge double canoe inside a bamboo and reed shelter on Vava'u sketched in 1838 by LeBreton.

O T A G O.

Otago, described by Capt. Cook as a chief on Tongatapu drawn by William Hodges in 1777.
Note that his little finger has been amputated, a sign of mourning in ancient Tonga.

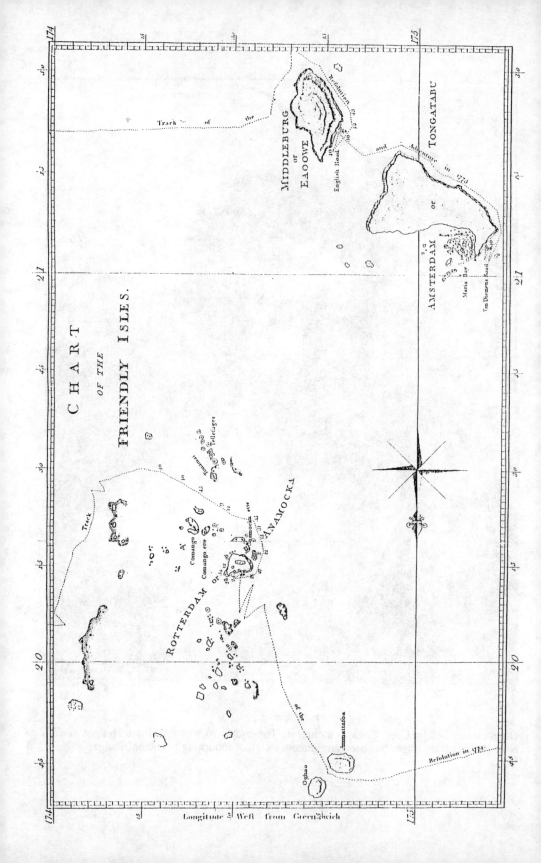

Tongan canoe sketched by Piron, artist on the Dentrecasteaux expedition of 1800.

DOUBLE CANOE OF THE FRIENDLY ISLANDS

Interior of a Tongan temple in Vava'u drawn during D'Urvilles visit in 1838.

A windy scene in Vava'u harbour sketched by LeBreton, D'Urville's artist in 1838.

Nomuka Island (Rotterdam) of Tonga drawn by William Hodges during Cook's visit in 1774.

A VIEW IN THE ISLAND OF ROTTERDAM

"Establishment of Master Thomas" on Vava'u, Tonga, by LeBreton in 1838. Note kava bowl.

Tongan men and a traditional house, circa 1910.

Tongan women pose in a photo studio, circa 1910.

Tongan women at a Missionary function, circa 1920.

CHAPTER 2

THE MYSTERY OF THE POLYNESIANS

*Let us not look back in anger
or forward in fear,
but around us in awareness.*
—James Thurber

The settlement of the Pacific remains a mystery to this day. The vastness of the Pacific as well as the lack of concern by historians has made tracing the origin of the Polynesians, at best, difficult. While anthropologists agree that there are at least three races in the Pacific region, they have not agreed on where they came from or when the Pacific was settled.

Evidence now suggests that man may have ventured out into the Pacific over 30,000 years ago. New discoveries in partially submerged caves in New Ireland, a long narrow island east of New Guinea are proving that man reached these islands tens of thousands of years ago.

In his book *The Fragile South Pacific*[46] Andrew Mitchell says "Until recently archaeologists who worked in the Bismarcks and the Solomons were unable to find any evidence of occupation by man older than 4,500 years. This seems odd, for man appears to have been in mainland New Guinea for at least 40,000 years; indeed some believe that agriculture originated in the highlands of New Guinea, so old are the cultures that have been discovered there. What took man so long to reach these nearest major islands? ...In 1985, Jim Allen and Chris Gosden from La Trobe University in Melbourne, excavated Matenkupkum cave in New Ireland and found human artifacts 33,000 years old deep in the earth deposits. These finds are set to revolutionize theories about the movement of man into the Pacific."

According to Maori tradition, the first Maori to come to New Zealand was the warrior Kupe, a powerful man and a legendary navigator of Pacific. Kupe was fishing near his island home Hawai'iki,

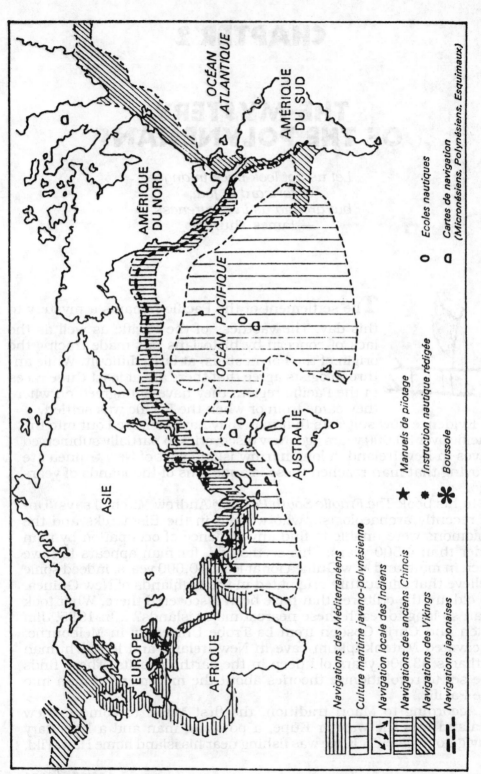

Pierre Carnac's map of ancient maritime voyages, including a Javanese-Polynesian empire of the Pacific.

when a great storm arose and blew him far down to the south, where he sighted Aotearoa, "the land of the long white cloud." The legend says that Kupe eventually made the return voyage to his homeland, and told them of his discovery. Many researchers believe that this happened as late as 950 A.D., but other theories place it much longer ago than that.

At one point, the ancient homeland of Hawai'iki got overpopulated, and a huge wave of migration set out for Aotearoa in ten great canoes, supposedly in the 14th century. The names of the canoes are still remembered in the stories, and their landing points, crews, and histories are also recalled. Even today, many Maoris still trace their history back to one of these ten canoes.[66,73]

It is generally accepted that Maoris are Polynesians, but the location of Hawai'iki is open to considerable interpretation. Most anthropologists who write about the Maori do not believe that Hawai'iki is the same as modern day Hawaii. Rather, accepted belief usually places Hawai'iki at either Tahiti or in the Marquesas Islands east of Tahiti.

Carbon dating in New Zealand places settlements there at least about the ninth century A.D. In addition, according to tradition, New Zealand was already inhabited by another race of people before the Maoris, a group of people called the Moriori. The Moriori were driven out of New Zealand and lived only on the remote Chatham Islands, which are more than 500 miles to the east of New Zealand.

Portait of a Marquesan chief drawn in 1784 by Capt. Cook's artist Hodges. The tattooing on the face suggests a script, not unlike shorthand.

Early observers to New Zealand considered the Maoris and Moriois to be different ethnic groups, though today prevailing theory is that they were part of different waves of "Polynesian" migration, the Moriois being part of the earliest migratory waves. Today, with the discovery of the Kaimanawa Wall in the Taupo district of the North Island, there are indications of even earlier settlers in New Zealand than the Moriois.

Since archaeologists admit that nearby islands to New Zealand such as Tonga, Fiji and New Caledonia were colonized at least 3000 years ago, it seems that these same navigators would have reached New Zealand as well. The history of New Zealand, and many Pacific islands, would seem to need some radical revision.

Early Theories on the Polynesians

The origins of the Melanesians or the origins of the Micronesians, while mysteries as well, has not occupied historians as much as the origins of the Polynesians. The origin of the Polynesians perplexed early explorers in the Pacific from the very start. The Dutch Navigator Jacob Roggeveen said that the Polynesians were descended from Adam though "human understanding was powerless to comprehend by what means they could have been transported to the Pacific."[66] Such doubts also afflicted James Cook and his men.

Prior to the publication of Darwin's *The Origin of the Species*, it was generally believed (by Europeans anyway) that the races of man were descended from the sons of Noah, Shem, Japheth and Ham. Darker races were considered the sons of Ham, while lighter races,

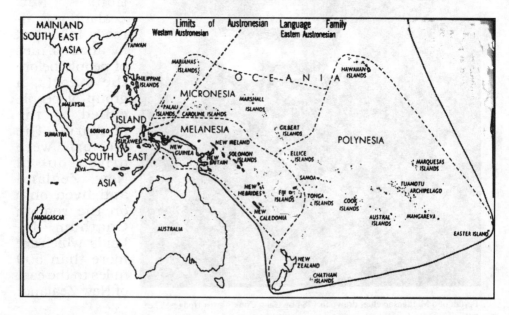

such as American Indians and Polynesians, were considered the sons of Shem.

Early on, a Malaysian origin for the Polynesians was speculated. The second edition of pioneer anthropologist J.F. Blumenback's book *Natural Varieties of Mankind* (1781) added a fifth race to his originally speculated four of Caucasian, Asiatic, American and Ethiopian. This fifth race was Malaysian, which included the Polynesians.[66]

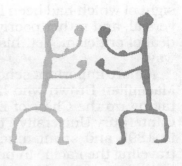

With the arrival of missionaries in the Pacific came other theories, such as that the Maoris "had sprung from some dispersed Jews," thereby making them one of the lost tribes of Israel. We now have the notion that Maoris, and Polynesians in general, are Semites. The *Book of Mormon* also follows this theory, stating that the Polynesians were descended from American Indian Semites who first landed in Hawaii in 58 B.C. after voyaging in Mexico and South America. Thor Heyerdahl has sought to provide some evidence this hypothesis in a number of his expeditions. Heyerdahl is not a Mormon, but does believe that there was contact between Polynesia and the Americas. Heyerdahl has stated that voyagers in the Pacific came from both the shores of Asia and the Americas. Many critics of Heyerdahl have believed that he advocates the American contact theory exclusively, which is wrong.

Archaeologists admit that there is evidence that the Polynesians were in contact with North and South America, especially such island or groups as the Marquesas, Rapa Nui and Hawaii. The sweet potato plant, or yam, is originally from South America and was known to have been cultivated on many Pacific islands before European discovery. The South American sweet potato was cultivated in ancient New Zealand and the Maoris called it Kumara.

However, contact with the Americas does not necessarily mean that the Polynesians originated there and the prevailing theory of the late 1800s and early 1900s was that the Polynesians were actually an Indo-European group who came to the Pacific via India. Linguistic evidence was usually cited, such as the detection of Sanskrit words in Polynesian vocabularies. In the days when racism was a common fact of life, one reason for such a theory was partly political: to prove that a fellowship existed between Maoris and Europeans. The main contributor to this theory was a book entitled *The Aryan Maori*, by Edward Tregear, published in 1885.[70]

Tregear postulated that the Maori were descended from the warlike, pastoral Aryans; that the Maori language preserved "in an almost inconceivable purity" the speech of his Aryan forefathers and had even "embalmed" the memory of animals and implements, the sight of which had been lost for centuries. His theories were controversial, and rather poorly presented, so they naturally drew a great deal of criticism. Yet, his was to become the dominant theory anyway.

A more important scholar who supported Aryan Maoris was John Macmillan Brown who had studied at Glasgow and Oxford before taking up the Chair of English, History, and Political Economy at Canterbury University College in 1874. Brown retired from his chair in 1895 and spent much of the remaining forty years of his life traveling the Pacific in pursuit of his intellectual hobbies, including the origin of the Maori. Brown settled in New Zealand and published his first book, *Maori and Polynesian* in 1907.[68]

A leading philologist of his day, Brown stressed that the "true classification of linguistic affinities is not by their grammar, but by the phonology."[68,66] Unlike earlier philologists, Brown admitted that the phonology of the Polynesian dialects differs by a whole world from that of all the languages to the west of it—that is, the language of Melanesia, Indonesia, and Malaysia. How then did the Aryan forbears of the Polynesians come into the Pacific?

Brown believed that they had come by several routes from the Asian mainland. Some had come through South East Asia, having been driven on by a Mongol influx, others had come in a northern arc through Micronesia. This northern migration had passed over the Bering Strait into the Americas before doubling back to colonize eastern Pacific islands like Easter Island. The Polynesian language that eventually emerged was a combination of several primitive Aryan

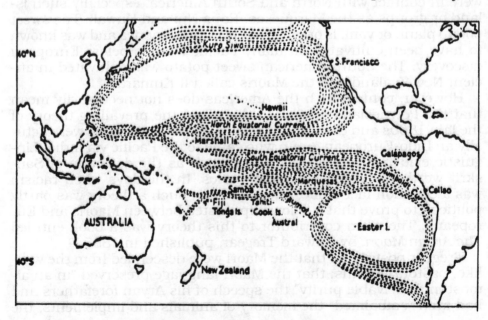

Map of Pacific currents.

A Tongan tongiaki canoe.

tongues. In *Maori and Polynesian* Brown suggested that the amalgam was formed in Indonesia, but later he shifted his ground. In his 1920 thesis, *The Languages of the Pacific,* Brown argued that "the linguistic attitude" of the Polynesians faced "north towards Japanese and Ainu." What had induced Brown to change his mind was the discovery of Tocharish, a "primeval" Aryan language as Brown called it, in a manuscript found at Dunhuang in the Gobi Desert in 1911. This famous cache of ancient texts, some written in unknown languages that have never been deciphered, was to provide a gold mine for those scholars who took interest in them.[66,67,68]

Said Brown, "The main features of the Polynesian tongue... go back to the old stone age in Europe....We must conclude that the Aryan language started on its career from twenty to twenty-five thousand years ago, and that philological students of Latin and Greek and the modern European languages must study Polynesian in order to see the type from which these sprung."[66,67]

Brown went on become Chancellor of the University of New Zealand, and enthusiastically championed unorthodox theories on the origin of the Polynesians, even to the point of advocating a lost continent in the Pacific which a few years later was called "Mu" by Colonel James Churchward. Brown found Greek, Celtic, and espe-

cially Scandinavian models for Polynesian gods. He found in the demigod voyagers in Polynesian traditions—in Whiro, Kupe, Turi, and Tangiia, for instance—a reminder of the "half mythical Scandinavian Vikings who sailed to Iceland and Greenland and Finland."

Brown had traveled widely throughout the Pacific, something most anthropologists and historians had not done, and was awed by the many megalithic remains he had seen. He believed that he could trace the footsteps of the Aryans into and through the Pacific from their megaliths. Brown claimed that the megalithic remains at Coworker and Atiamuri in New Zealand were evidence of Aryan occupation.

Brown's magnum opus on the Pacific startled many people. His final book, *The Riddle of the Pacific,*[1] published in 1924, claimed that there was once a continent in the Pacific that was now mostly submerged. This continent, of which most Pacific islands were the last remnants, had been founded by Aryans from America.[69] Here was the Chancellor of the University of New Zealand advocating a sunken civilization in the Pacific and not without reason. Brown may have first become convinced of a lost Pacific continent when he was introduced to the ancient texts at Dunhuang. One of the ancient papers allegedly contained a fragment of a map which showed a sunken continent (see my book, *Lost Cities of China, Central Asia & India*[16]). Brown had also been to Easter Island where the local tradition has it that natives are from a sunken land called *Hiva*. He was convinced that an advanced culture once existed throughout the Pacific and that sudden cataclysms had submerged most the land causing a collapse of the civilization.

Despite the fact that geologists of his time discounted any rapid geological change in the Pacific it is a fact that the flat-topped guyots throughout the Pacific must have been formed above the water. These wind-blown mesas, similar to those in the American southwest, need thousands of years of blowing sand to flatten their tops. Similarly, large atoll archipelagos such as the Tuamotus, Kiribati or the Ha'apai group of Tonga would become mini-continents if the ocean levels were dropped only a few hundred feet. Today, geology remains divided as to slow geological change and sudden geological catastrophes that occasionally take place. Most geologists now favor both theories and admit that occasional catastrophes do take place, just how often is the usual question.

Hawai'iki, the Birth Place of Maui

The notion of a lost continent in the Pacific was not taken seriously by most historians, but the notion of an Indo-Aryan origin for Polynesians certainly was. One historian was Stephenson Percy Smith, founder of *The Polynesian Society* in 1891. Smith used notes he had gotten from a high Rarotongan priest named Te Ariki-tara-are to trace the Polynesians back to India, though he admitted that the Indian side of it was weak through lack of records in India. He created the following table for the Aryan migrations to the Pacific:

450 B.C.	India
65 B.C.	Java
450 A.D.	Fiji-Samoa
650 A.D.	Hawaii
675 A.D.	Marquesas
850 A.D.	Maku visits New Zealand
1150 A.D.	Toi visits New Zealand
1175 A.D.	Moriori move to Chatham Islands from mainland
1250- 1325A.D.	Voyages to New Zealand of Maori forerunners.
1350 A.D.	New Zealand settled by "The Fleet" of ten canoes.

Today, evidence is showing that it is most likely that New Zealand was populated long before 850 A.D. Smith was unaware of the Lapita Pottery discoveries to come decades later proving that early settlers reached western Polynesia by at least 1200 B.C., therefore his estimate of 450 B.C. was overly conservative as is his entire time table.

In the 1840s in the North Island of New Zealand, Reverend William Colenso was given a metal bell by local Maoris who had been using it as a cooking pot. Maoris were not known to work metals, and they claimed to have found it at the base of a tree. An inscription in archaic Tamil-Dravidian, from which the Tamil language of southern India is derived (it precedes Sanskrit) is on the bell. It reads: "Bell of the ship Muhamed Buks." The name "Muhamed" is an ancient name, used in ancient India and the Middle East. The bell is now kept at

A comparison of a Hawaiian helmet and an ancient Greek helmet.

the Wellington Museum.[73] Because of this ancient bell, many early anthropologists believed that ancient Hindus commonly voyaged to New Zealand and Pacific, something the ancient Hindus probably did as seen in the surviving remnant of Bali.

At one point in prehistory, starting around 1500 B.C., the Hindu-Nagas of India and Southeast Asia spread into the Indonesian archipelago creating a sophisticated island nation based on Hinduism, elaborate ritual and seafaring as far as the edge of New Guinea. The ancient Hindu maritime empire extended from Pakistan and Iraq to Java, Bali, Borneo and beyond. The Hindu island of Bali is all that remains of this great empire now, but formerly it may have ruled many islands in the Pacific.

Another theory cropped up at the turn of the century, this one classifying the Maoris and Polynesians as belonging to the Alpine section of the Caucasian race and located their primeval home in the Atlas Mountains of North Africa. The late Barry Fell, founder of the Epigraphic Society, maintained that the Polynesians were North African sailors who worked as a hired navy for the Egyptian pharaohs.[76]

Elsdon Best in his book *The Maori*, published in 1924, said that according to Maori traditions, they came from a western land called Uru and

Part of a broken monolith from Malekula, New Guinea.

then migrated to Irihia which, he said later, was very like Vrihia, the Sanskrit name for India. Another famous anthropologist was New Zealander Peter Buck, half Maori, whose Maori name was Te Rangi Hiroa. He also accepted the Indian origin of his ancestors and wrote in his book *Vikings of the Pacific*[15] in 1938: "...in remote ages the ancestors of the Polynesian people probably did live in some part of India." Then they worked eastwards through the river courses of South East Asia into Malaya and Indonesia where the pressure of Mongoloid people "turned their gaze to the eastern horizon and embarked upon one of the greatest of all adventures."

Still, according to tradition, Maoris and all Polynesians came from Hawai'iki. Yet, as the modern scholar Margaret Orbell echoed the views of other anthropologists, Hawai'iki was considered a place from which Maui, the ancestor of man, came and to which the spirits of the deceased returned. Therefore, Hawai'iki was regarded as the source of man, of all men, and of food, plants, customs and even knowledge. So when Maoris were asked where they came from, they replied that they came from Hawai'iki. Moreover, Hawai'iki could be located to suit the occasion: in the east, the direction of the rising sun, for the beginning of life; to the west, as the setting of the sun, for death and the departure of spirits. Orbell concluded that Hawai'iki was not the name of an historical fatherland but a supernatural place of much importance in the religion of Polynesians.[66]

Egyptians In the Pacific

The late Professor Barry Fell, a former Harvard Professor and native New Zealander popularized the theory that the Pacific was settled in second millennium B.C. by the Egyptians. He is well known for advocating Egyptian, Libyan, Celtic and Phoenician ancestry for American Indians, and applies his epigraphic (the study of ancient writing) research to Polynesians. Says Fell in his popular book *America B.C.*[76] after linking Libyan language to the Zuni Indians, "These phonetic rules are of the same kind as another series I demonstrated in 1973, linking the Libyan language with that of Polynesia. The Polynesian people, like the Libyans themselves, are descended from the Anatolian Sea Peoples who invaded the Mediterranean around 1400 B.C. and, after attacking Egypt and suffering a series of defeats as the Egyptians record, eventually settled Libya. Later the Libyan seamen were employed by the Pharaohs in the Egyptian fleet, and still later the Libyan chiefs seized control of Egypt to establish the Libyan dynasties. Thereafter Libyan influence spread far and wide, especially in the Indo-Pacific region, where the Egyptians mined gold, as in Sumatra. During the Ptolemaic period (after Alexander the Great conquered Egypt) Libyan seamen in the service of the Greek Pharaohs explored widely, some of them settling parts

Characters Used in Oleai Written by the Chief Egilimar.

na	tschra	rä	
goo	mmä	lüh	P N Runge
dâa	tschä	sthah	
Bä	moâ	töo	X EYE
tschroa	TO	wä	B RoU N
nôo	ma	schä	HGNEX
pui	boa	kä	EGILIMAR
Tu	tä	soä	
ma	pä	bag	————
Bö	vôa	ku	The mark ^ indicates accent
mä	schrü	schrä	
ngä	pu	gkaa	
boa	lö	rü	
warr	tät	nga	
râa	va	môo	
uh	lä	gä	
dôo	moi	du	

of the Pacific."

According to Fell, "The foregoing inferences, based largely on linguistic studies, have forced us to discard the theory that traced the Polynesian settlements to supposed immigrants of uncertain origin in East Asia, for the early Polynesian inscriptions are essentially Libyan both as to the alphabet and the language. Linguists such as professor Linus Brunner in Europe and Dr. Reuel Lochore in New Zealand have found this new interpretation to be consistent with their own researches into the sources of the languages of Malaysia and Polynesia (see Brunner and Schafer's, *Malayo-Polynesian Vocabulary*, Auckland, 1976). It also explains the occurrence of Greek words in the Polynesian tongues. As Professor Brunner has pointed out, the Greek colonies in Libya used a dialect of Greek in which certain consonants replace those of Attic Greek, and it is in the Libyan form that the Greek words of Polynesia occur. The Anatolian elements in Polynesian have been the special study of Lochore, and these too are now seen to be consistent with a Libyan origin of the Polynesians, for we know from the ancient Egyptian records that Libya was settled by the Anatolian Sea Peoples."[76]

Therefore, what Fell is saying is that he believes that the Polynesians were descended from Libyans in the service of Egypt, working as sailors to Egyptian gold mines in Sumatra, and even Australia and elsewhere. He also believes that many Melanesians are the descendants of Negro slaves used as workers in the gold mines. Fell even goes on to call the dialect used by the Zuni Indians of the American south-west as *Mauri script* and maintains that the Maoris may be related to the Zuni Indians and their "Mauri" language.

Phoenician and Libyan rock inscriptions have been discovered in

Indonesia. A letter in the January 21, 1875 issue of the magazine *Nature* spoke of Phoenician script in Sumatra. Writes the author, J. Park Harrison: "In a short communication to the Anthropological Institute in December last (*Nature*, Vol. XI, p. 199), Phoenician characters were stated by me to be still in use in South Sumatra. As many of your readers may be glad to have more information of the subject, I write to say that the district above alluded to includes Rejang, Lemba, and Passamah, between the second and fifth parallels of south latitude. Several manuscripts, on bamboo, from this region are preserved in the library of the India Office; and a Rejang alphabet is given by Marsden in his *History of Sumatra,* third edition. Some of his characters, however, appear to have been incorrectly copied. About half the Refang letters are admitted by all the Oriental scholars to whom I have shown them to be Phoenician of the common type; others being similar to forms found in Spain and other Phoenician colonies. Most of the letters are *reversed,* a peculiarity which is explained by the fact that the Rejang writing, according to Marsden, is read from left to right, contrary to the practice of the Malays generally. The matter is of great interest, and, it is to be hoped, will be investigated by Phoenician scholars."[83]

Over the many years of modern archaeological research a great deal of evidence for Phoenician and Egyptian mining operations in Sumatra, Australia and into the Pacific has accumulated. It is likely that the Egyptians, Phoenicians, Dravidians, Cambodians and Chinese all came into the area of Australia and the western Pacific.

Circa 1000 B.C., King Solomon's Phoenician ships made a three year trip across the Indian Ocean to a land of gold called Ophir. The theory is this: by 4,000 B.C. and probably much earlier, the Egyptians were sailing across the Indian Ocean to Sumatra, Australia and New Guinea. They mined gold and traded with Indonesians, explored Australia and exploited it's vast resources as best they could, and continued across the Pacific in a joint Hindu-Egyptian colonization and commercializa-

Trobriand Islanders in the Torres Straits of New Guinea with highly prized amphlett pots for preparing taro.

tion of the Pacific and ultimately with the advanced cultures of North and South America.

The question that arises is "Where is the evidence for such a claim?" Fortunately, the evidence is overwhelming, particularly when one realizes how easy it is to sail across oceans in even the crudest of boats if one has courage and knowledge of basic star navigation. The Egyptians in fact had large and sophisticated navies.

One clear link between Australia and Egypt is that the Torres Straits Islanders, between New Guinea and Northern Queensland, use the curious practice of mummification of the dead. The Macleay Museum at Sydney University has a mummified corpse of a Darnley Islander (Torres Strait), prepared in a fashion that has been compared to that practiced in Egypt between 1090 and 945 B.C.

It was reported in Australian newspapers circa 1990 that a team of Marine archaeologists from the Queensland Museum had discovered extensive cave drawings on many of the Torres Straits Islands. Some of the cave drawings, on isolated Booby Island, were of a Macassan prau which is a unique vessel with telltale double rudders and triangular sails used by beche de mer (sea cucumber) fishermen out of the Indonesian island of Sulewesi. The archaeologists declared the Torres Islands the "crossroads of civilizations" and were quoted as saying "Now it's a new ballgame in an archaeological sense."

In 1875 the Shevert Expedition found similarities in Darnley Island boats and ancient trans-Nile boats. The island boats were used to row corpses to sea and leave them on a coral reef. Egyptian practice was to ferry corpses across or down the Nile for desert burial.

Similarly, it was pointed out by the Kenneth Gordon McIntyre in his book *The Secret Discovery of Australia* (Picador, 1977) that the island of Mir in the Torres Strait was similar to the Egyptian word for pyramid, "mir" and even that the name for Egypt is "Misr." Another similarity with the Torres Strait Islanders, as well as in the Solomon Islands, Fiji and Polynesia, a wooden headrest was used. This carved headrest was used to slightly elevate the head, while the subject slept on

Drawing of typical Phoenician galley of 1200 B.C.

his back. It is unusual to ancient Egypt and certain Pacific Islands around New Guinea that these headrests are used.

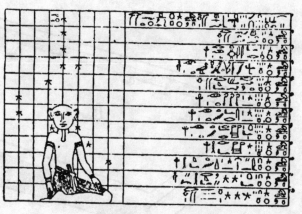

Ramesside Star Clock

Curiously, on the island of Pohnpei (formerly called Ponape), the new capital of the Federated States of Micronesia, an ancient Egyptian word is important in the government. Pohnpei island is divided into five districts and the governor of a district is called a Nan-marché in the language of Pohnpei. Similarly, in ancient Egypt, a district was known as a nome, and a district governor was known as a nome-marché. Here we have the exact same word meaning the exact same thing in ancient Egyptian and modern Pohnpei dialect. A coincidence?

The Egyptians built their ships without nails, and a number of ancient ships, many without nails, have been found along the coasts of Australia. Two ships 40 feet long and 9 feet wide, built without nails, have been found near Perth, Western Australia. Another was found partially hidden underneath a sandune at Wollongong, New South Wales.

On the Atherton Tablelands of Queensland in 1910, Mr. A Henderson dug up a Ptolemy IV coin from the Ptolmaic period of Egyptian history, 221-204 B.C..

At Ipswich, Queensland in 1965 workmen dug up a cache of hand-forged Egyptian bronze, copper and iron tools, pottery and coins dating back more than 2,000 years.

At Rockhampton in 1966 an Egyptian calendar stone, gold scarabs, and gold coins were found. Also in Queensland, near Herberton, can be found rock paintings that apparently depicting a two stem papyrus, the swamp plant of ancient Egypt. A three stem papyrus rock painting can be found near Mareeba.

At the Gympie Museum (Queensland) can be found a three foot tall rock statue of a baboon holding a papyrus against his chest. It was discovered in the 1920's on a farm near Gympie, near what was said to be a terraced, pyramidical hill. The Egyptian god of science, Toth, was typically depicted as a baboon. Baboons only live in Africa (and parts of Arabia).

In a sand dune at Austinmer, New South Wales in about 1930 a woman found a handmade silver necklace and bronze armband re-

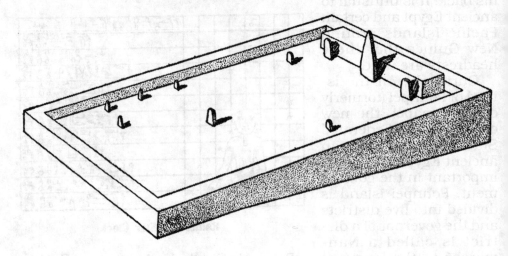

Tahitian marae platform with standing stones.

ported to be of ancient Egyptian origin. In the vicinity of Austinmer gardeners and beachcombers have found gold figures, pottery fragments, scarab beetles and small Egyptian figures.

In Western Australia, around 1914, half-way between Perth and Geraldton, 100 miles inland, Mr. H. E.Thomson found Egyptian lotus flowers growing on recently burned ground. The Curator for the Perth Botanical Gardens identified them as lotus plants foreign to Australia.

In the town of Geraldton in 1963 workmen excavating 28 feet below the sea bed brought up an Egyptian bronze plate form an ancient beach level.

In the Sydney suburb of Ryde in 1969 a gardener dug up hand-forged fragments of iron pottery inscribed in the Egyptian style.

In the Sydney suburbs of Fivedock and Campsie, gold coins and ancient Egyptian jewelry have been dug up.

At Towradgi a 2,000 year-old coin was found in a sand dune. Near Goulgburn, a farmer plowed up an Egyptian silver coin.

Near Newcastle a broken bronze sword, earthenware pottery fragments, and old copper coins have been dug up, near remains of stone dwellings and a stone wharf. At Campbelltown an image apparently of an Egyptian deity is cut into a cliff face.

Half-way between Sydney and Newcastle Egyptian-like hieroglyphics are cut into a rock face. Nearby, very old aboriginal rock art shows Egyptian-like figures.

The anthropologist Elizabeth Gould Davis says in her book, The First Sex (G.P. Putnam's Sons, 1971), "In Australia was found a pendant amulet of greenstone, carved in the shape of the Celtic cross, an exact duplicate of an amulet found in Egypt at Tel el Amarna, the site of the ancient city where Nefertiti and the Pharaoh Akhenaten held court thirty-five hundred years ago."

The French researchers Luis Pauwels and Jacques Bergier say in their book, Eternal Man (Souvineer Press, 1972) "In 1963 a strange and disconcerting piece of information came to us from Australia. A pile of Egyptian coins that had been buried for about 4,000 years was found in terrain sheltered by rocks. The readers who gave us this information referred to some rather obscure reviews for there was no mention of this find in any archaeological publication. However, the widely-read Soviet review Tekhnika Molodezi which devotes a regular column to unexplained facts with comments on them by experts took up this matter. It even published photographs of the excavated coins."

Other Mysteries of the Western Pacific & Australia

In an article in the prestigious journal New Scientist that was entitled "Pacific Islanders were the First Farmers," (*New Scientist*, Dec. 12, 1992, page 14) author Leigh Dayton points out that archaeologist J. Golson, formerly of the Australian National University, has found ditches and crude fields in this area. The implication is that humans were tending plants here between 7,000 and 10,000 years ago.

The article further points out that on Buka Island in the Solomons, while excavating Kilu cave, archaeologists M. Spriggs and S. Wickler unearthed small flake tools with surfaces displaying starch grains

The Tahitian pyramid temple of Mahaiatea.

and other plant residues. Evidently, these tools were used for processing taro. Further, the starch grains resembled those of cultivated rather than wild taro. The date for find was an astonishing 28,000 years before present! The article points out that a site at Wadi Kubbaniya, Egypt has been dated at 17,000 to 18,000 years old by G. Hillman of the Institute of Archaeology, London. This site also had grinding stones and tuber remains, but the Solomon Island discovery was 10,000 years older!

Another new discovery is that of a pyramid and stone sphinx on a remote island off of New Guinea. It is known to a nearby logging company, but not to the outside world in general. This giant pyramid has only been seen by helicopter and by a few natives of the island. It may have been the main island trading port for the Egyptian and Hindu presence of the early Pacific.

No one yet knows the age of this pyramid and "sphinx" on a remote island near to the Solomons. Recent geological tests on the famous Sphinx of Giza has shown that the solid-rock statue has been underwater for a long period of time and must be many thousands of years old. Could the sphinx of the Solomon Islands be 10,000 years old or more?

When some of the more than 400 gravel hills on New Caledonia were excavated in the 1960s, they had cement columns of lime and shell matter that was carbon dated by Yale and the New Caledonia Museum as having been made before 5120 B.C. and 10,950 B.C. These intriguing cement columns can be found in the southern part of New Caledonia and on the Isle of Pines.

A major colony in the timber and metal rich Solomon Islands would make an excellent sea colony to explore and trade across the Pacific. Here we find a connection with the Aroi Sun Cult and pyramid building religion of the Polynesians. Their sacred island and cult center was Raiatea, where they built massive platforms and step pyramids by the sea, and erected gigantic statues.

Many Easter Island statues have an Egyptian ankh at the base of their spine. Each of the statues re-erected at Anakena Beach by Thor

Solomon Islands canoe in Suva Harbor, Fiji.

Heyerdahl has a large ankh carved on it's back, at the base of the spine. This motif would also seem to symbolize the kundalini power of the spinal column.

There is a cave painting in the Prince Regent River Valley in the Kimberleys of Western Australia which includes a man with a beard and tall hat, looking very Middle Eastern or Egyptian in origin. Around him are three women with long hair that is tied at the end. These women have been identified as Egyptian dancers with weights at the end of their hair. Their long, weighted hair was an intricate part of their show.

Similarly, the Egyptians used boomerangs just as Australian Aboriginals. The Egyptians frequently hunted ducks in the marshes of the Nile with boomerangs, as well as played games with them. It is an archaeological fact (though not well publicized) that a trunk full of boomerangs was discovered in 1924 when King Tutankhamen's tomb was opened by the archaeologist Howard Carter. Many of these gold and lapis lazuli inlaid boomerangs are on display in the Tutankhamen exhibit at the Egyptian museum in Cairo, and next to them is an Australian boomerang for comparison.

Boomerangs were also used in Texas, Arizona, Northern Mexico and California. It is an interesting thought that the Australian Aboriginals, as well as tribes in the American Southwest, learned the use of the simple but ingenious boomerang from the Egyptians!

Numerous books have been written that have touched on the subject of Egyptians in Australia. Some are biographies of well-known Australians, such as Sister Ruth by Victor C. Hall (Neville Spearman, London, 1968) This book was about an outback nurse and the wife of a local Mounted Policeman, Ted Heathcock, who lived and worked with Aboriginals in the Northern Territory during the 30s and 40s. A portion of the book concerned her experiences at the "ruined city of the moon," at the Brimmy Valley in the Rose and Roper River areas of the Northern Territory. The place is called "Burrangie" by the natives, a secret place of the giant people who belonged to the Dreamtime, a legendary time of Australia's dim past.

Another similar book was *When Strange Gods Call* by A.M. Duncan-Kemp (Brisbane, 1968) which was the autobiography of the wife of rancher in far northwestern Queensland. She talks about, and has photos of, strange ruins in the Northern Territory. She also writes about similari-

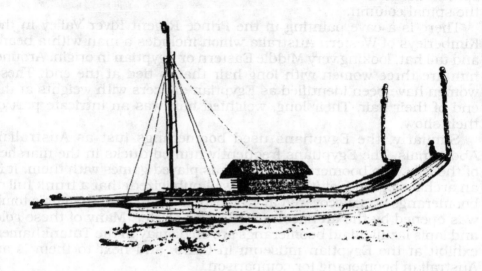
Sketch of a Tahitian double-canoe from Cook's third voyage in 1777.

ties to certain Aboriginal customs and signs to that of the Masons and Egyptians.

The book *The Secret Discovery of Australia* by Kenneth Gordon McIntyre (Picador, 1977) is largely about early Spanish, Portuguese and Dutch exploration, also mentions early Hindu and Arab exploration and that the island of Mir in the Torres Strait was similar to the Egyptian word for pyramid, "mir."

In the Corgi paperback novel *The Ibis Seal* by Anne O'Grady (Corgi, 1975) the romance-adventure plot centers around an Egyptian settlement in the far north of Cape York, Queensland that is being excavated by an archaeologist obsessed with proving that Egyptians had been the first explorers to discover the vast continent. Because of many valuable Egyptian artifacts being found, and a lost treasure, the book ends in considerable murder and mayhem.

Early Chinese and other Voyages

There is also the very possibility of early Chinese, Arab, Greek and even Mayan and Incan voyages into the Pacific. In his book *Millennia of Discoveries*,[31] historian Alexander Adams maintains that the Greeks made voyages into Indonesia and the Pacific. Says Adams, "In the fourth century B.C., energetic King Philip II reorganized Macedonia and established it as a capable military power that would dominate the Greek policies of the future. His son, Alexander the Great, by destroying Thebes broke up Greek resistance for many years. The brief but illustrious career of Alexander put his name in history books forever. In eleven short years he demolished the giant Persian empire and Macedonian and Greek soldiers marched to the borders of India.

"After his death in 323 B.C., the Hellenistic Age began. Rapid Hellenization of the Near East allowed Greeks to settle there in big numbers and exploit trade with East Africa, India, and the faraway China.

"The Macedonian fleet explored the Indus River and the southern coasts of modern Iran, Pakistan, Oman, and the gulf states. Understanding the principle of the monsoon—tropical winds in the Arabian Sea—allowed Greeks to sail directly from the Red Sea across the Arabian Sea to India. The need to follow the coasts of Arabia disappeared.

"The Macedonian dynasty of Ptolemies ruled Egypt from 323 to 30 B.C. Relying on the knowledge of the ancient Egyptians, the Ptolemies monopolized the Red Sea trade and became primary suppliers of pearls, gold, ivory, slaves, and papyrus to the Greek markets.

"Greeks fleets left Egypt and followed the African coast to the African horn and rounded it, sailing down south along the East African coast. These journeys took them all the way down to modern Mozambique and Tanzania, where traded with the Sabean communities. What was the extent of the Greek travels? Either most of the ancient Minoan and Mycenaen heritage was totally forgotten by the fourth century B.C. or some of it was never known to the Greeks. But their own travels established them as pioneers in their own right.

"Modern Hawaiian and Polynesian contain some Greek words, suggesting that certain Greeks sailed way past India to the Pacific. Greek coins have been found in Java and in southeast Asia."[31]

In his book *Lost City of Stone*[39] historian Bill S. Ballinger theorizes that a fleet of Greek ships ventured out into the Pacific after the death of Alexander the Great and ended up founding a dynasty on the remote Micronesian island of Pohnpei. They built the gigantic ruins of Nan Madol on the southeast corner of Pohnpei, and explored much of the Pacific with their large Greek ships, based out of Nan Madol, Ballinger's "Lost City of Stone."

Similarly, Chinese voyagers into the Pacific have been the subject of a number of books. Says Alexander Adams in *Millennia of Discoveries*,[31] "The Chinese have many legends of the long journeys across the Pacific. The Chinese refer to certain Tien-mu Mountains about seven thousand *li* to the east. A *li* equals three miles, which makes these mountains about twenty-one thousand miles away.

"Considering a little exaggeration, it points to mountains located half a world away, nevertheless. In the third century A.D. a Chinese wrote: 'East of the Eastern ocean lie the shores of *Fusang*. If, after landing there, one travels East for 1,000 li he will

come to another ocean, blue in color, huge and without limit.'"[31]

This other ocean is apparently the Caribbean, an ocean that is deep blue in color. Chinese expeditions arrived in California, journeyed across the deserts to the Gulf of Mexico, and even visited the Grand Canyon.

According to archaeologist Henriette Mertz in her book *Pale Ink*[41] the Chinese made several recorded voyages across the Pacific and some of these voyages were recorded in well-known Chinese books such as the 2250 B.C. book known as *Classic of Mountains and Seas* and the book *Fu Sang* written by a Buddhist missionary about 400 A.D. Many Chinese expeditions were sent into the Pacific, such as an expedition in 219 B.C. which never returned to China. Some Chinese sailors and expeditions may have settled on Pacific Islands in Micronesia and Polynesia, perhaps eventually intermarrying with Polynesians in Samoa, Tonga and Tahiti. Some Chinese ships had five decks for passengers plus cargo space and some of the first-class cabins were equipped with bathrooms and running water.

Says Alexander Adams, "When Spaniards reached the Pacific coast of Mexico and California, they reportedly talked of seeing the wrecks of Chinese junks there. There is also corroboration of Chinese stories coming from the Americas. Indian tribes in the Pacific Northwest talk about visitors in the great ships from the west. Their baskets are typically Asian. In the eighteenth century A.D., during his voyages along the coast of the Northwest, Captain Cook described the boats of the natives. These boats had sails that folded in the same manner as did the sails of the Chinese junks.

"The hollow mulberry tree is called fu-sang in China, and Chinese called the land across the ocean Fu-Sang. The Chinese visited Fu-Sang many times and described its laws, people, and customs. All these

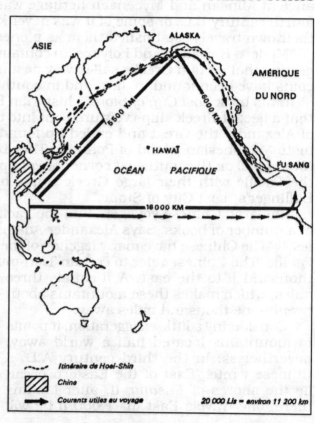

Pierre Carnac's route map for Chinese voyages to Fu Sang.

descriptions pint to Mexico."[31]

Adams also discusses the spread of various ancient board games, "It is interesting to trace the travels of the board game was widespread from India to Crete, and Polynesians had a similar game. In Mexico this game was known by the name Pattoli."

Egyptian explorers, early Hindus and Chinese voyages, similar Mayan expeditions and the mystery of the Polynesians is ongoing investigation. As archaeological discovery and dating techniques become more and more sophisticated, a further vindication of these theories may come about. Meanwhile, Pacific Archaeology continues to struggle against the early archaeological prejudices that influenced it such as the erroneous dating of many the megaliths.

The Erroneous Dating of Marquesan Megaliths

Who were the great megalith builders of the Pacific? Evidence now shows that that the Pacific was settled at a very early age, many thousands of years ago. Many of the stone monuments in the Pacific are now known to be much older than originally presumed by archaeologists.

One example of this the erroneous dating of the Marquesan megalithic platforms by the American archaeologist Suggs in the 1950s.

The Marquesas Islands are full of gigantic platforms, called *ahus*, just like in Easter Island. Throughout the islands, mysterious ruins covered in jungle can be found, testifying to a great, and vanished civilization. In Herman Melville's book, entitled, *Typee*,[98] a book about his own personal experiences as a castaway in the Marquesas Islands in 1842, we find interesting reference to the megalithic pyramids or platforms in the Marquesas: "One day in returning from this spring by a circuitous path, I came upon a scene which reminded me of Stonehenge and the architectural labors of the Druid."

Melville states, "At the base of one of the mountains, and surrounded on all sides by dense groves, a series of vast terraces of stone rises, step by step, for a considerable distance up the hillside. These terraces cannot be less than one hundred yards in length and twenty in width. Their magnitude, however, is less striking than the immense size of the blocks composing them. Some of the stones, of an oblong shape, are from ten to fifteen feet in length, and five or six feet thick. Their sides are quite smooth, but though square, and of pretty regular formation, they bear no mark of the chisel. They are laid together without cement, and here and there show gaps between. The topmost terrace and the lower one are somewhat peculiar in their construction. They have both a quadrangular depression in the center, leaving the rest of the terrace elevated several feet above it. In the intervals of the stones immense trees have taken root, and their broad boughs stretching far over, and interlacing together, support a canopy almost impenetrable to the sun. Overgrowing the greater part of them, and climbing from one to another, is a wilderness of vines, in whose sinewy embrace many of the stones lie half hidden, while in some places a thick growth of bushes entirely covers them. There is a wild pathway which obliquely crosses two of these terraces; and so profound is the shade, so dense the vegetation, that a stranger to the place might pass along it without being aware of their existence.

"These structures bear every indication of a very high antiquity, and Kory-Kory, who was my authority in all matters of scientific research, gave me to understand that they were coeval with the creation of the world; that the great gods themselves were the builders; and that they would endure until time shall be no more. Kory-Kory's explanation, and his attributing the work to a divine origin, at once convinced me that neither he nor his countrymen knew anything about them."[69]

Melville then goes on to offer his opinion that these and other megalithic remains on the island are the work of an ancient and extinct race, and are not the work of the Marquesas Islanders that we know today. He even hints at the submergence of lost lands in far antiquity. However, several archaeological expeditions to the Marquesas were done in the 1950's by the American archaeologist Robert Suggs who related the discoveries in his 1962 book, *The Hidden Worlds of Polynesia.*[71]

Suggs' excavated a platform on Nuku Hiva in 1956 at Hikouku'a in the Hatiheu Valley on the northern coast. It had two large stone statues, and a massive platform called a *tohua*, or ceremonial plaza. They were constructed of coarse, dull red volcanic tuff. The site had long been concealed from western visitors. Suggs and his crew found inside

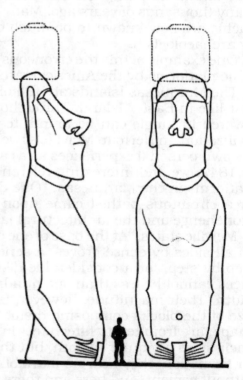

A comparison of the largest of statues at Rapa Nui with a man.

the massive boulder pile such artifacts as a Civil War musket, a French Brandy bottle, and a glass bowl manufactured in Philadelphia in the late 1700's. All of these things indicated to Suggs that the platforms had been constructed since the arrival of Europeans to the Marquesas. This was termed the "classical period" by Suggs.

Despite the fact that Melville had clearly described the massive platforms as something that were not newly built, but of such antiquity that the people had no oral history of it and his Marquesan guide described them as being "coeval with the creation of the world." It would seem that Suggs has fallen into the trap of other archaeologists in that after finding "datable objects" around clearly undatable megaliths, he was tempted to date the megaliths by objects that had been placed inside the large gaps hundreds if not thousands of years after they had been built. Strangely for these "scientists" it did not even occur to Suggs that the objects, clearly of recent European or American manufacture, had been placed in the platforms during recent burials or ceremonies. It is an amusing thought to think that one of the artifacts may possibly have even been one of Melville's!

Orthodox archaeologists have often stuck to the 1860 (approximate) date of the Marquesan platforms, yet modern archaeologists are now mostly aware that the platforms are much older than suggested by Suggs. These objects were clearly placed between Suggs estimated that they began construction about the year 1400 and continued up to late 1800's.

Suggs, on the other hand, was convinced that these platforms had just been constructed, and even, because of the American Civil War musket, that they were still in the process of being constructed in the mid 1800s! Melville's book was actually published in 1846, almost two decades before the American Civil War!

That the platforms may have actually been constructed hundreds, if not thousands of years before, is not even suggested in his book. Suggs at least admits that the actual construction of the blocks is a mystery. Says he, "It would naturally have been impossible for us to have completely excavated and dismantled so huge a terrace, which supported the remains of about twenty buildings, all of them constructed of massive stones."[71]

Suggs does have some interesting things to say about the Marquesas, however. He was particularly interested in dating Marquesan civilization, and was able to utilize carbon dating methods for the first time in any Marquesan archaeology. Suggs believed

that the Marquesas were occupied as early as 120 B.C., while the conventional date is usually around 300 A.D. Suggs also believed that the Marquesas were settled from a well-equipped expedition from Tonga or Samoa.

The typical goggle-headed Marquesan statue has often been compared with Chinese Bronze-Age statues. Suggs felt the statues were far more recent, and rejected any connection. He was also opposed to Thor Heyerdahl's theories of diffusion from South America, saying that no Peruvian pottery or tools have ever been found in Polynesia. But many of the goggle-headed Marquesan statues are also found in Peru and Bolivia, particularly at the ancient Tiahuanaco site or at Chavin, both civilizations over 5,000 years old!

Legends of Viracocha & Quetzalcoatl in the Pacific

Another curious between China and the Americas is the presence of an avatar-figure on both continents who apparently made the voyage from Asia to South America across the Pacific, no doubt stopping at Polynesian islands along the way.

The South Americans have legends of Viracocha, a foreign "god" who came across the Pacific to teach the people about love and brotherhood. Says Adams in *Millennia of Discoveries*,[31] "He was associated with the color white and was the sun god. The same deity is revered by Buddhists and is called Vairochana. The symbol of Buddha, the lotus, was found depicted in the arts of the American Indians. Buddhists in China were called 'the sons of Skaya.' In the Mexican highlands, priests of very high rank were called Tay Sacca—"men of Sacca." Many words of ancient India and Tibet written in Sanskrit (an Indo-European language) are also found in the languages of Amerindians. Traditions of royal customs of China can traced in Mexico and Peru.

"The Chinese emperor was called the 'Son of the Sun,' and Inca rulers in Peru called themselves by the same epithet. When Chinese royalty died, their servants were buried with them. The same custom is found in Peruvian burials. Masks with protruding fangs were typical of China and have been found throughout Mesoamerica and the Andes."[31]

An interesting tale which relates to ancient Polynesians and ancient seafarers is the story of Wakea which is told in L. Taylor Hansen's fascinating book, *He Walked the Americas*.[74] L. Taylor Hansen was the daughter of the coauthor of theory of continental drift, the Taylor-Wegner theory, and she collected tales of a bearded white man variously called Viracocha or Quetzalcoatl who walked all over North and South America preaching and healing people.

Hansen wrote a letter to Dr. Peter Buck, then the director of the Bishop Museum in Hawaii, and asked him: "Do you know of a prophet or teacher who came among the Polynesian Islands, teaching theology and agriculture? He dressed in a long white toga-like garment. His eyes were grey-green, his long light brown hair had reddish highlights, and he was bearded. If you recognize this figure, please tell me his name, his century, and the manner of his coming. From which direction did he arrive, and whence take his departure? That is, if your legends can answer these questions."

Dr. Buck's reply was, "I recognize this figure from our legends. His name is Wakea. The other questions I cannot answer, much as they intrigue me. However, I am to go to an outlying island of the Tahitians where two old women can still chant the ancestor-legends. From them, and another in a different island, I hope to learn the answers. Therefore, in two or three months you will hear from me again."

In three months, as promised, came the second letter.

"Wakea, the Healer, lived in the first century of the Christian Era, or generally speaking, in the time of Jesus. It seems that he came in the early dawning of our history to these tribes who were fighting in this outlying island. The white god of Polynesia was evidently a human being coming in three Roman-type ships from the direction of the Red Sea and could definitely be assigned to the Century of Christ, plus or minus some fifty years. I am enclosing a copy of the story as it was told to me."

A comparison of three similar scripts: Indus Valley writing, Rongo Rongo script, and Linear A script from ancient Crete and Greece.

Hansen goes on to tell the story sent to her by Peter Buck, half-Polynesian himself. "To an island where men were fighting for the possession of the good land came three ships with giant sails like enormous birds with wings up-lifted, glowing goldenly in the dawn-light. Suddenly frozen to immobility were the warriors as the ships moved around a jutting headland.

"Forgotten was the heat of the battle. Friend and foe stood facing seaward, weapons clutched in paralyzed fingers, staring in wide-eyed wonder.

"The ships' oarsmen, whose paddles looked like a hundred centipede legs touching the water, rested now from their task of moving the giant monsters forward.

"Then the islanders saw something white moving toward them. Apparently it had come from the Great Birds, and it glided easily over the water with rhythmical ease of a man walking.

"As the spot of white came closer, they saw in amazement that this was a Fair God, man-like in form, but unlike their people. Soon they could see Him clearly, the gold of the dawn-light shining behind and around Him, making a halo of His long-curling hair and beard. They saw the foam-like swish of his garments. As *He* came up on the wet sand, the warriors stared in fright at His garments; they were dry. Now they knew that a god stood among them, for none but gods can walk on water!

"From His garments, so foam-white, they looked to his pale face and then into His eyes. They were strange eyes, grey-green as the depths of the water, and like it, ever changing. Now those eyes flashed with anger as he stared about him and looked upon the injured.

"A god had come from the sea to walk among them and his first look was that of anger! The warriors fell down as one man and began an old chant anciently employed to a god for forgiveness. When they dared again to raise up their own eyes, they saw *Him* going among the injured and dying who arose from their pain to find themselves well of body as soon as His hand or His garments had touched them.

"Thus on this never to be forgotten day came the beloved Wakea to live for awhile among the people."[74]

Hansen goes on to relate Buck's story, that Wakea signaled the ships and other men came ashore who like Wakea, were bearded. The strangers returned to their ships after some days, but Wakea remained with the Polynesians. They then took him to each island, where he preached of the One God who ruled the Heavens. To Him, war was not of His making, for His law was *Love One Another*. For Wakea, the people gave up war and the sacrifice of children which kept down their populations so they would not overeat their islands.

Then one day, after Wakea had visited all of the islands, Wakea asked about the lands to the east. "The people were not entirely unacquainted with the continent lying eastward. Did they not have the yam to eat, and call it by its ancient South American name? Yet they were loathe to lose the healer, this strange god who answered to the name they had given him: Wakea, the Fair God Of The Ocean."[74] And so, according to L. Taylor Hansen and Peter S. Buck, the ancient teacher, Wakea, journeyed to South America in the Polynesian "Boats of the Migrations" where he became Viracocha.

The Maoris of New Zealand have commemorated the event of Wakea with an etched glass window at the *Te Hahi o te Whakaono,* The Church of Faith, in Rotorua. At the church, sandblasted on plate glass, is a figure of Wakea walking on Lake Rotorua. He is wearing a Maori Korowai cloak, the type worn by a chief, adorned with kiwi feathers. This was the first Christian church in Rotorua, capital of the Maoris. It seemed only fitting that Wakea be etched in the glass, creating the illusion of a man walking on the lake just outside the window. Perhaps he had done just that on the same lake nearly two thousand years before.

The Land of Giant Birds & the Tuatara

Ancient Polynesia was a strange land of giant birds taller than a man, weird dinosaur-lizards called the Tuatara, vast forests, giant bats, and all manner of weird sea life. Ancient Polynesia spanned many large and small islands but the great southern island of New Zealand was Polynesia's great frontier with its vast mountains and forests.

New Zealand boasts many unique animals including the most bizarre of all, the tuatara *(Sphenodon punctatus),* the sole survivor of the order of Rhynchocephalia, a lizard which paleontologists say predates the dinosaurs. The tuatara is a unique animal on the face of the earth, and exists in its own "order." The tuatara is a large olive-green lizard, some 2 feet, 3 inches long, which still has a vestige of a third eye on the top of its skull. This is called the pineal eye and is found in the higher vertebrates in the shape of the epiphysis or pituitary gland.

That this relic, "older than the dinosaurs," still exists in New Zealand is perhaps evidence of an ancient continent in the Pacific. Indeed, to explain some of the animals in New Zealand, certain geo-

Drewing of a moa.

logical concepts of continental drift and vanished continents were formulated.

More interesting still is the moa, one of the largest birds that ever existed. One interesting theory about the dinosaurs that has gained increasing popularity over the years is that dinosaurs, like birds, were warm blooded. In this theory, birds are then the natural ancestors of the dinosaurs. In other words, dinosaurs did not become extinct, they evolved into birds. The first birds can be found in New Zealand, the kiwi for instance. It has hairy feathers and vestiges of wings. The kiwi is also the only bird with its nostrils at the end of its beak. The moa, however, had no vestige of wings at all. There is no sign of a collarbone by which a vertebrate's front legs are almost invariably connected to the thorax. It is the truest of bipeds, and its feathers are so primitive that they seem more like hairs.

Some moas were twelve feet tall and lumbered around the forests of New Zealand like small dinosaurs. Others were only the size of a small turkey. Moas dwelt in the forests by the hundreds, and the first Polynesians to arrive called them simply "moa," their word for common fowl. Yet by the time the first European explorers arrived, the moa was practically, if not entirely, extinct. Only the nocturnal kiwi still thrived. Curiously, a flightless megapode bird called the *Megapodius pritchardii* lives on the island of Niuafo'ou in far northern Tonga. This bird is similar to the kiwi or the dodo bird of Mauritius. Is it a last surviving megapode bird that once existed in other parts of Tonga? Ancient Tonga may have had large flightless birds just as New Guinea, Australia and New Zealand.

Says Andrew Mitchell in his book A Fragile Pacific, "The distribution of megapodes in the Pacific is very odd. They are found in northern Australia's forests and scrublands, throughout much of Southeast Asia, and in New Guinea. Aeons ago it seems that they progressed down the Solomon Islands land bridge with relative ease— one species reached the New Hebrides further to the west, now know as Vanuatu—and then they apparently vanished, only to reappear on one single island in the middle of the Pacific Ocean, the Island of Niuafo'ou in the Tongan group. The *Megapodius pritchardii* lives in splendid isolation surrounded on all sides by vast expanses of ocean."[46]

The question of why Moas died out has led to a lot of arguments, ever since the first discovery of moa bones in the 1830s by a trader, Joel Polack, soon after the British anatomist Richard Owen had surmised that such a bird once existed. Mummified moa remains were discovered along with rock carvings, and some Maori chiefs still remember the Moa hunting songs. But, what had created such a monster bird, and similarly, why was it that similar giant flightless birds, such as ostriches and rheas, also existed all over the world, and how did they get there? Did they evolve independently, or somehow together?

The generally accepted theory is also a controversial one. This theory is well summed up in the book, *No Moa* by Beverley McCulloch published by the Canterbury Museum in Christchurch.[75] Ms. McCulloch says, "The islands of New Zealand are often regarded as Pacific Islands and part of Polynesia. Geologically, however, they are quite distinct from most of the islands of the Pacific. New Zealand is in fact a piece of a continent, like Australia or Africa, only a small portion of which emerges from the ocean."

Is Ms. McCulloch speaking of a sunken continent? No! She is speaking of the breakup, theoretically 150 million years ago, of the super continent of Gondwana. She continues, "This piece of continent was once part of the great southern continental land-mass called Gondwana. Millions of years ago Gondwana broke up and pieces drifted apart to become Antarctica, Africa, South America, Australia and India, and the islands of Malagasy and New Zealand. Each piece took with it, like a huge Noah's Ark, some of the plants and animals which grew and lived in Gondwana."

Says McCulloch, "Most of New Zealand's flightless and poorly-flighted birds probably lost their flying ability after the land was isolated as an island. In a situation where there is plenty of food and it is on the ground, there is little point in wasting energy on flying, particularly when there are no enemies from which to escape. But the ancestors of moas and kiwis certainly walked here. We can be sure of this because moas and kiwis have so many relatives in other broken-up bits of Gondwana, as for example the ostriches of Africa, emus of Australia and rheas of South America. All are closely related and all are flightless; it is clear they descended from the same flightless Gondwana ances-

Drewing of a moa.

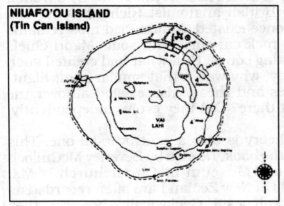

NIUAFO'OU ISLAND
(Tin Can Island)

tor. Their differences developed once the pieces of Gondwana, each with its little community of marooned, walking birds, drifted off into different parts of the globe."[75]

This is the standard Gondwanaland drift theory of the distribution of megapode birds around the world, though it has been pointed out that the Pacific is its own continental plate and can't be having other continents "drift" over it. Rather, a subduction zone would be created, as indeed there is at the Tonga Trench on the western side of the island group. A great deal of volcanic and earthquake activity occurs at this trench and this is the site of a number of appearing and disappearing islands.

The main problem with most Gondwanaland theories is that they were developed before the geological theory of tectonic plates became widely accepted. Therefore, Gondwanaland is a jigsaw puzzle that is missing a few pieces, namely the Pacific tectonic plate. According to tectonic plate theory, these giant plates rub against each other, rise and fall, and can go under another plate, creating a "subduction zone." Conversely, they can pull apart, much as in the theory of Gondwana, creating what is called "ocean floor spreading."

The Pacific tectonic plate is neither a subduction zone or an ocean floor spreading zone. It is a genuine plate of crust, the largest in fact, and has subduction and spreading zones all around it. These zones generally make up what is known as the "Ring of Fire." Therefore, Gondwanaland continental drift diagrams should take into account the Pacific plate, certainly above water 150 million years ago. What is more, oceans have continental plates as well, so, generally speaking, it is impossible for continents to just drift all over the world, going where they will. They won't go too far without colliding into another plate, even if it is submerged. When this happens, either a mountain range or subduction zone is created.

The only theory that accommodates the Gondwanaland drift theory as originally proposed is the *Expanding Earth* theory first expounded in 1933 by the German geologist Hilgenberg. He proposed that as the earth sphere expanded the continents originally had fit together and had pulled apart as the earth expanded. Except for the expanding globe, his theory correlated closely with Gondwanaland theories.

All of the large flightless birds, known as *megapodes*, belong to a group known as ratites. Yet to say that these birds lost their ability to fly over thousands (millions?) of years does not ring true. For one thing, the moa has not even the vestige of wings! Even seals and whales still have vestiges of arms and feet. It appears that the moa never flew and was never meant to. Nor does its lack of wings explain why it became extinct, after all, Africa, Australia, New Guinea and South America are teeming with giant flightless birds, no better off in terms of wings than the moa. Why shouldn't they be extinct? After all, they were and are hunted by men as well.

The answer to that question would appear to be that moas, and the aepy- ornis or elephant bird of Madagascar, became extinct (if they are) because they were ultimately trapped on relatively small islands (compared to continents, anyway) where they had a limited space in which to run from pursuers.

Perhaps moas are the best example of dinosaurs turned into birds, lumbering along on huge, powerful legs, they merely stepped on animals that gave them a hard time, after all, they weren't bothering anybody. Then along came man with his spears and arrows, and suddenly moas couldn't kick and stomp those that would do them in.

Then there is the tuatara, last ancestor of some bizarre, primitive reptile. Where are his relatives? Lost beneath the Pacific Ocean or deep frozen under a mile of ice in Antarctica in the last poleshift?

While some sort of Gondwana may well have existed in the remote past, it seems that in more recent times (dare I say 24,000 years ago?) moas and other animals, including woolly mammoths, diprotodons, giant ground sloths and the like, were roaming the vast continent of the Pacific, including New Zealand. Also, perhaps the displacement of giant, flightless birds, as well as marsupials in North America and giant land tortoises in the Galapagos and Indian Ocean, could be explained by a now sunken land mass in the Pacific.

Yet, could it be that moas are not even extinct? Ivan T. Sanderson reports in his book, *More Things*,[78] that in 1967, because of the discovery of several live Takahe in 1950, a colorful, flightless bird believed to have been extinct for for over half a century, a government naturalist visited the forested fjordlands of the South Island in an official capacity. His duties included actual exploration of these vast unmapped mountains and the surveying of an enormous wildlife reserve.

This area is uninhabited and not crossed or even penetrated by hunters or others. It was the last retreat of a certain small subtribal group of the *Early Maoris* who were driven from fertile lowlands to the north by a combination of the *Later Maoris* and the early white colonists. The government naturalist reported after visiting this area that he had seen definite, concrete, fresh evidence of the continued existence of a small species of moa during his trip. However, he did not want to be quoted or to have his name used in published accounts.[78]

This report of evidence of still living Moas is backed up by another report in 1960 of the sighting of a live moa in the same area by another trained zoologist. Both parties particularly desire that their official reports be not issued to the public, because they have no photographic proof or plaster casts of the spoor they say they found. Sanderson goes on to tell of other cases of moa bones discovered in 1949 showed that the bird had obviously been butchered and eaten; some of the bones had a series of very fine deep cuts that could probably only have been made only by a metal knife.[78]

Sanderson then theorizes that it is possible that small bands of Early Maoris still survive in the vast wilderness of the fjordland, along with some moas. Do the ancient Moa Hunters of old New Zealand still live on, continuing their ancient traditions? The idea is too much for most people, and even the idea of small forest-dwelling moas is generally scoffed at.

The incredible lost world of megalithic pyramids, giant birds, huge lizards and romance of ancient seafaring continues today in the legends and monumental remains throughout Polynesia.

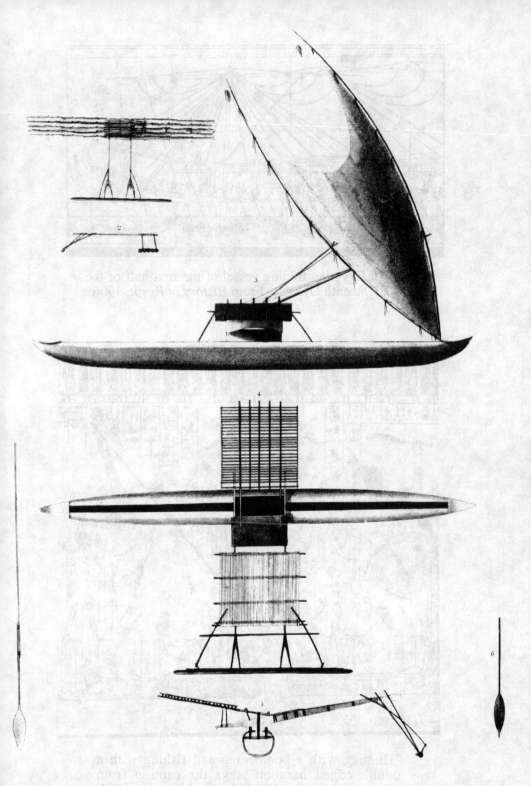

Plan of a canoe recorded at Vanikoro in the southeast Solomon Islands during the voyage of
L'Astrolab, 1826–29 (D'Urville 1833).

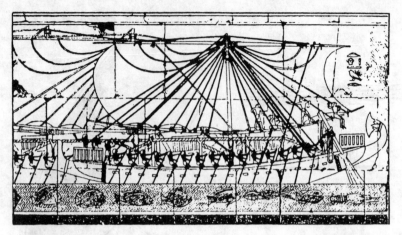

An Egyptian trading vessel of the first half of the
Eighteenth Dynasty. From *History of Egypt*, 1906.

"Hunting with a boomerang and fishing with a
double-edged harpoon" says the caption from
History of Egypt, Vol. 2, by G. Maspero, 1906,
The Grolier Society, London.

Amber-glass obelisk-shaped pin found in a field at Kyogle Australia in 1983. It is said to be 5,000 years old.

Two statues dug up near the Hawkesbury River, NSW. The man on the left is bearded. Both seem to be of ancient Middle Eastern Manufacture, and are said to be of Phoenician origin.

A sketch by George Grey in 1841 of a cave in the Kimberley Mountains of northwest Australia. Note the Wandjina drawings and that the stones in front of the cave appear to be cut and squared.

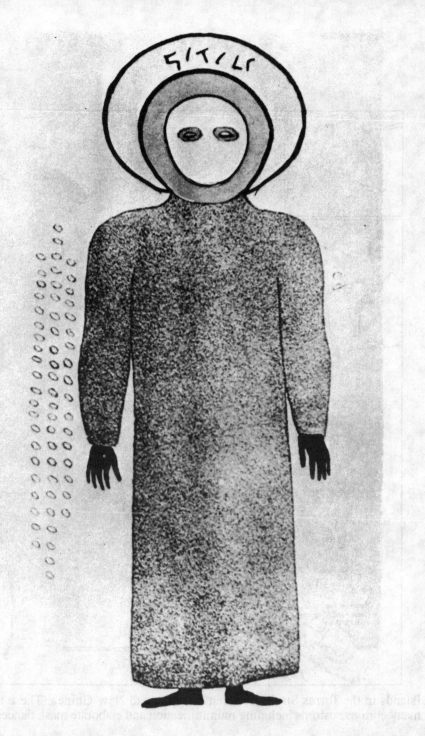

George Grey's sketch in 1837 of a Wandjina figure from the Glenelg River in the Kimberley's of northwest Australia. The figure wears a long robe and has a type of script above the head, a script similar to ancient Phoenician or Hebrew.

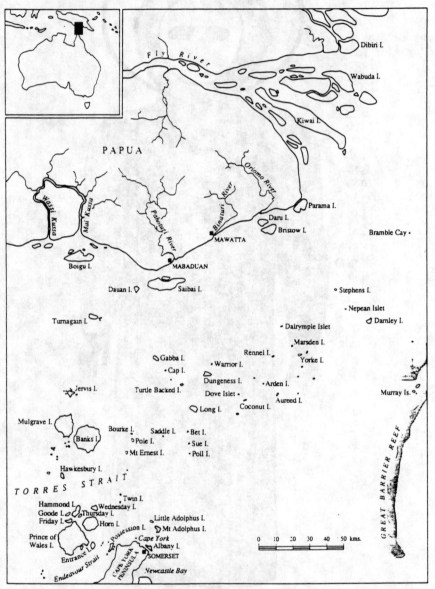

Islands in the Torres Straits between Australia and New Guinea. These islanders had many curious customs including mummification and elaborate mask dances.

A. C. Haddon photographed this masked dancer on Thursday Island in 1888. He was taking part in a ceremony to welcome the arrival of the monsoon. The head-dress includes both native and European materials. (Reproduced from volume 4 of the *Reports of the Cambridge Anthropological Expedition to Torres Straits*.)

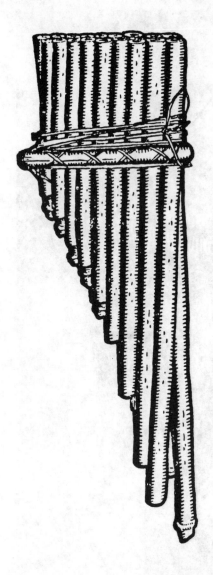

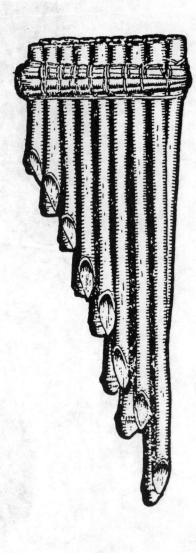

Panpipes from the Solomon Islands (left) and Bolivia.

Two illustrations from a Peruvian history book. Top: The Inca Tupac Yupanqui's expedition to the Marquesas and Tuamotu Islands in balsa rafts. Bottom: A double-hulled reed ship used in the Pisco area of Peru.

Two balsa rafts from Quayaquil, Ecuador. Top: From 1748. Bottom: From 1843

Contemporary drawings of the monumental remains on Rapa Nui (Easter Island). Above: Rapa Nui has huge walls that are similar to those in Tonga. This fine wall is Vinapu, often said to have identical construction to walls in Peru. Left: An islander stands next to one of the giant long-eared statues. These statues are buried up to their chins in soil, a testimony to great age.

Hawaiian in a feathered helmet and cloak, drawn in 1784. His feathered helmet is virtually identical to the military helmets worn by Greeks and Romans. Could he be the descendant of Greek or Libyan sailors? Kahuna tradition says Hawaiians came from Egypt.

Sound	Style of Tunisia and Numidia	Style of Libyan settlers of Iowa	Style of Libyan voyagers in Pacific (Ancient Maori)
b	⊙, ⊡	⊡	⊡
g	V, ∧	V	Γ
d	⊏	F	⊏
w	‖	‖	‖
z	ᴟ, —	ᴨ	—
t̪	ᴟ, ⅄	ෆ	⊓
k	⇑		↓, ⇓, ⇑
l	=, ‖		=, ‖
m	⊔, ⊐	∪	∪
n	∣	∪ ∣	∪ ∣
r	○, ⊅, ▢, ◁	○	○, ▢
š	W	⋀	
A, '	∙, ◁		(, ∙,)
t	✕, +	✕	✕, +

Libyan inscriptions employ the above alphabet, but the language is nearly the same as that of Ancient Egypt. The language was first deciphered from North African bilingual Latin-Libyan tombstones by Fell (1973). Thus the Iowan text, originally found in 1874 and later condemned as a forgery, is in fact genuine, for it could not possibly have been forged. Other Libyan inscriptions have been found in Quebec, New Hampshire, Pennsylvania, and Oklahoma. They also occur on Pacific Islands and in Chile. On linguistic grounds Fell derives the Polynesian language from ancient Libyan (with some Anatolian and Asian elements). In North America the language of the Zuni Indians is also derived from ancient Libyan, and occasional Libyan alphabetic signs occur in Zuni art. Ancient Libyan was also written in the Mimbres valley in New Mexico 700 years ago.

From *America B.C.* by Barry Fell.

Tattooed Maori chief from the last century. Facial tattoos were popular in New Zealand, the Marquesas and Easter Island.

Left: According to Maori legend, the God Pourangahua flew from his legendary dwelling place of Havaiki to New Zealand, seated on a magic bird.

An alignment of upright slabs on Necker Island in Hawaii.

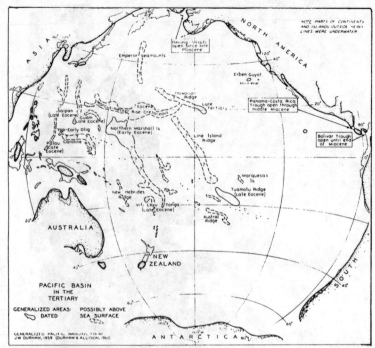

An interesting speculative map from "Paleogeography of the Tropical Pacific" by H.W. Menard and Edwin Hamilton included in *Pacific Basin Biogeography; A Symposium* published by the Bishop Museum in 1963.

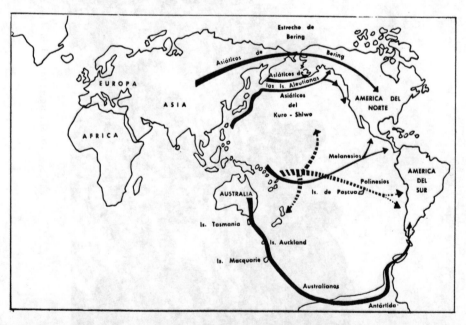

One concept of the settlement of the Pacific and South America by the Peruvian anthropologist José Busto. It is an unusual concept, not only because he acknowledges ancient trans-Pacific contacts, but even theorizes the use of Antarctica as a land-bridge. From the book, *Peru Preincaico (Pre-Inca Peru)*, Lima, Peru, 1985.

One of the platforms from the north coast of Malden Island. Courtesy of Bishop Museum.

Another photo of a ruined platform, looking southwest. What was the purpose of all these platforms? Were they part of an ancient Sun-Worshipping Empire that stretched throughout the Pacific many thousands of years ago? Was Malden Island a central meeting place?

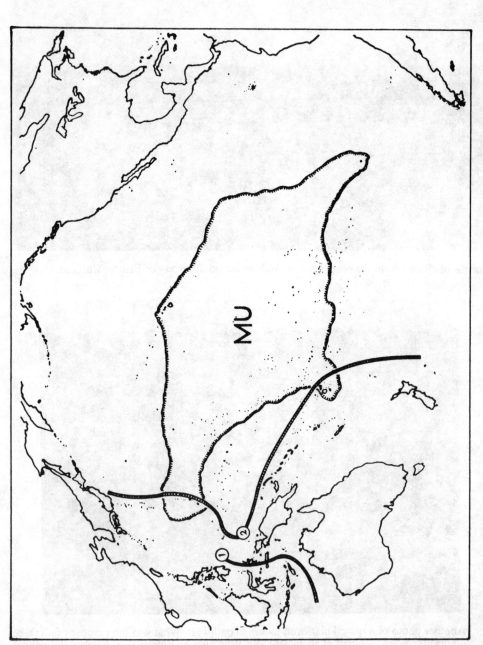

MAP OF THE PACIFIC OCEAN, showing (1) Wallace's Line, (2) the Andesite Line, and Churchward's lost continent of Mu.

The great British anatomist, Richard Owen, with his version of how a moa went together. There has always been a tendency to assemble moas so that they were as tall, and therefore as spectacular, as possible.

An engraving of the Moa and a kiwi from F. von Hochstetter's *New Zealand* . . . . . 1867, (pl. 176).

Herman Melville described the massive platforms of the
Marquesas in his book, *Typee*, published in 1846.

The great *paepae* at Vahangeku'a, Taipivai.

NUMEROUS WORLD AREAS BOAST OF BAREFOOT FIREWALKERS. THE FIJI ISLANDS' SAWAU TRIBESMEN ARE RATED THE MOST REMARKABLE PERFORMERS. THEY BUILD A CIRCULAR PIT LINED WITH LARGE FLAT STONES AND, OVER THEM, A HUGE LOG FIRE. TEN HOURS LATER THE LOGS ARE REMOVED. SHOUTING "VUTU-O," A LINE OF FIREWALKERS PARADES ACROSS THE RED HOT STONES, ANKLES CIRCLED BY TWIGS OF FRESH LEAVES. THEY COME THROUGH WITHOUT THE SLIGHTEST SIGN OF A BURN AND, STRANGELY, THE LEAVES ARE UNHARMED. IT'S STILL A MYSTERY TO SCIENCE HOW THIS IS DONE.

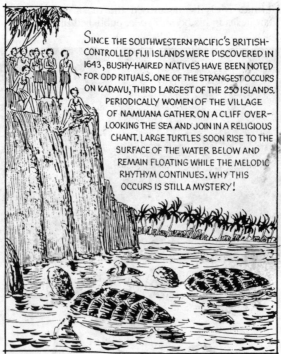

SINCE THE SOUTHWESTERN PACIFIC'S BRITISH-CONTROLLED FIJI ISLANDS WERE DISCOVERED IN 1643, BUSHY-HAIRED NATIVES HAVE BEEN NOTED FOR ODD RITUALS. ONE OF THE STRANGEST OCCURS ON KADAVU, THIRD LARGEST OF THE 250 ISLANDS. PERIODICALLY WOMEN OF THE VILLAGE OF NAMUANA GATHER ON A CLIFF OVER-LOOKING THE SEA AND JOIN IN A RELIGIOUS CHANT. LARGE TURTLES SOON RISE TO THE SURFACE OF THE WATER BELOW AND REMAIN FLOATING WHILE THE MELODIC RHYTHYM CONTINUES. WHY THIS OCCURS IS STILL A MYSTERY!

From *It's Still A Mystery*, by Lee Gebhart and Walter Wagner

CHAPTER 3

THE MYSTERIES OF FIJI

*The people of Fiji, Tonga and Samoa were all one 3000
years ago. The spoke the same language; they were a
single culture.*
—British Fijian archaeologist Simon Best

*Feejee and Tongataboo engage in war against each other;
and the inhabitants of the latter are often so much afraid of
his enemy that they bend the body forward and cover the
face with their hands, to express the sense of their own infe-
riority to the Feejee men...*
—Captain Cook in his journal

Fiji is currently the hub of travel for South Pacific islands like Tonga, Samoa, Vanuatu and Kiribati. Many visitors to the South Pacific will transit the modern airport at Nadi while on their way to one of the many island destinations surrounding Fiji. Was Fiji also a major island hub in ancient times?

Today Fiji is a mix between the South Pacific, Africa and India, with that touch of British culture that lingers in the former colonies. In recent years, the Indian immigrants brought in by the British have come to actually out-number the Fijians, a South Pacific people who were categorized as Melanesians. Yet, the ancient Fijians were once Polynesians, not Melanesians. Could Fijians be both Melanesians and Polynesians? Was Fiji once part of Tonga, or maybe Tonga once part of Fiji? At the time of European exploration in the Pacific the "frontline" in the war battle between Melanesia and Polynesia was the fine line between Tonga and Fiji.

The Origin of the Fijians

High on the northernmost slope of the Nakauvadra Range on Viti Levu, over 2000 feet up the slope where the mission grass ends and the thick rain forest begins, there is a knee-high stone with three holes cut deep into its side. The stone is called the vausososo. Villagers still place a small tuft of grass into one of the holes as did their ancestors for thousands of years, "To make the day longer and to satisfy the *vu*."[17]

Another 800 feet up the slope is the peak of Uluda, the sacred mountain of Nakauvadra, one of the traditional first settlements of Fiji. Near the peak of Uluda is where, according to local tradition, a chiefly voyager named Degei is said to have ruled over the cradle village, the original village of Fiji.

The Fijian legend states that a giant canoe named the *Kaunitoni*, carrying the God chiefs Lutunasobasoba and Degei, sailed from the ancient homeland and landed on the north-west coast of Viti Levu. The chiefs built their first village at Vuda, which means "our origin," but abandoned it, moving inland along a mountainous ridge which stretches from Vuda to Nakauvadra.

In "Kaunitoni Tradition" Lutunasobasoba died on the way to Fiji. Degei reached Fiji and landed at Uluda, "building the cradle village about five miles inland from the Ra coast near what is now Vatukacevaceva.

At the top of the peak of Uluda are two great stones known as the *rogorogo-i-Vuda*, sacred stones that were used to summon Degei from the first landing site of Vuda. From the top of Uluda it is possible to see as far as Vanua Levu.

Kim Gravelle of the *Fiji Times*, says that Degei is believed by many Fijians to be a man, a spirit and an ancestor. "In legends, Degei is an angry spirit who caused the ualuvu levu, the great flood which supposedly carried the first Fijians from Nakauvadra to all

Fijians in turbans climb the mountain of Vuda.

The hilltop fortress of Ulunikoro

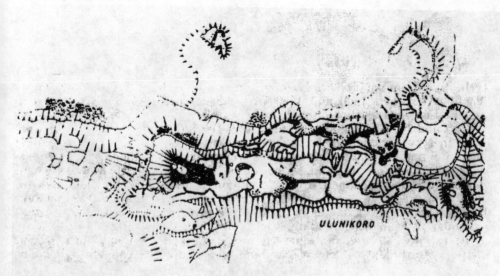

ULUNIKORO

parts of Fiji. In legends also, Degei took the form of a snake, inhabiting a cave near the top of Uluda."[17]

In the last century, Fijian warriors, guided by their priests, approached this cave on hands and knees and listened for a crash of war clubs which would indicate their success in an upcoming battle.

The Kaunitoni Canoe Theory

Anthropologists say that Fijians, like other Melanesians, migrated out of New Guinea to the islands nearby. However, it is actually taught in Fijian schools that the Fijians came during a great migration from Africa. This is called the "Kaunitoni Theory" after a type of canoe used in East Africa. Fijians are said to have similar customs to certain tribes in Tanganika. They are said to have come to Tanganika by way of Egypt and then crossed the Indian Ocean. Meanwhile the Malaysians were making a similar journey, though in reverse, to Madagascar. It is also said that the original homeland of the Fijians was Tirania in Central Asia and that from there they went to Egypt, then to Tanganika and on to Fiji.

One theory is that the Fijians are actually Nubians from southern Egypt and the Sudan. They were used as slaves and worked in the Egyptian gold mines in Sumatra and then later migrated to Fiji from those mines. The Libyan seamen who had transported the slaves to the mines, and the gold back to Egypt, in this theory, they migrated to New Zealand, Tonga and Samoa, and possibly Fiji as well. While this theory may work well to explain certain Melanesians in New Guinea and the Solomon Islands, it seems likely that the Fijians were of a separate migration altogether, perhaps a migration that

Fijian canoe with Mount Vuda in the background.

was multi-racial.

Is there any proof that Fijians have come from Africa as many have claimed? Well, one interesting thing about Fijian culture is that they use a wooden head rest as a pillow when sleeping, exactly as the Egyptians had. Traditional Fijian temples are built at pyramids. Otherwise, we only have the traditions of the Fijians themselves. But, if the Fijians did come to Fiji in giant canoes from Africa about 500 B.C., did they find the islands already inhabited?

The prehistory of Fiji is by no means clear. It becomes more and more of a mystery as more evidence becomes known. In the mid-1800's, missionary Thomas Willims spent more than a decade delving into Fijian oral history and wrote in 1860 that he had "sought in vain for a single ray of tradition" relating to the origin of the Fijians.

Says Kim Gravelle, "Other historian of the time had a similarly poor response, including a Land Claims commissioner who spent 20 years recording Fijian ancestry: he noted 50 legends, none of which mentioned Degei, Lutunasobasoba, or Vuda. And in 1865, missionary Jesse Carey sent a letter to teachers throughout Fiji asking them to record legends or beliefs of people in their areas. The replies listed the deeds of 300 gods and ancestors... but again, there was no mention of Degei, Lutunasobasoba, the Kaunitoni, or Vuda."

Gravelle says that the Kaunitoni theory of Fijian origins did not make its appearance until 1892, when a Fijian paper, Na Mata, ran a competition to trace Fijian origins. The winning entry said the people came from Thebes in upper Egypt and travelled up the Nile to Lake Victoria in Tanganyika, eventually migrating from Africa to Fiji, led by Lutunasobasoba on the Kaunitoni.

It is a startling theory, an Egyptian-African origin for the Fijians, though one has to wonder as to what it was that inspired these people to make such an epic voyage from Africa into the South Pacific. Such a journey would have required a journey across the Indian Ocean, through Indonesia, past New Guinea and Australia and into the vast Pacific. No small feat for any early navigators, yet a voyage that was very much possible. The ancient Malagasy had made a similar voyage in the other direction, migrating from the Malaysian peninsula to Madagascar many thousands of years ago.

The person who wrote the Kaunitoni story which won the history contest of 1892 had been schooled at the Navuloa Mission School where Gravelle reports that a text book in use at the time, written by missionaries, compared Fiji with Tanganyika on linguistic grounds and compared customs of Fiji with those at Thebes. Many researchers today believe that the Kaunitoni canoe belief is an invention of missionaries.

Despite the uncertainty of the origins of the Fijians, they must have come from somewhere. Lapita pottery found on Fiji is over 3000 years old, indicating the first Fijians, Degei, Lutunasobasoba, or whom-ever, arrived a long time ago. Fijians may well be from Egypt and Africa, and this may explain the curious fact that Fijians and Tongans speak the same ancient language in various dialects, yet are two distinct racial types. Egypt is a land that was inter-racial in ancient times, and would have had two different racial types speaking the same language. The Egyptians were known to have explored and possibly colonized along the East African coast and therefore it

Rock inscriptions near Dakuniba, Vanua Levu.

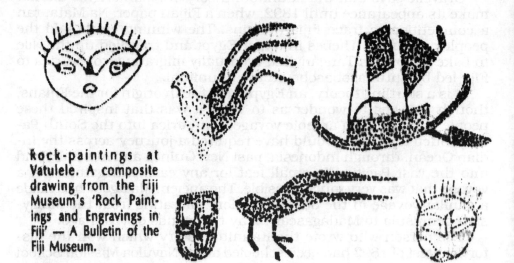

Rock-paintings at Vatulele. A composite drawing from the Fiji Museum's 'Rock Paintings and Engravings in Fiji' — A Bulletin of the Fiji Museum.

is quite possible that Fijian has some linguistic similarities with certain Tanganyikan dialects. If Fijian actually has some similarity to some East African languages, it would be interesting to see the evidence.

As far as the "Theban customs" used in Fiji, this may well be the use of wooden head stands for sleeping, an unusual custom used in Fiji, Tonga, Tonga and ancient Egypt. The Egyptians were also known for their excellent stone masonry technics, something that can be easily seen in Tonga and other Pacific islands, particularly Rapa Nui (Easter Island).

Lapita Pottery and Ancient Fiji

In 1975 British Archaeologist Simon Best began excavating a Lapita Pottery site at Lakeba near the village of Tubou in Fiji. Thermoluminescence dating of the pottery showed it to be approximately 3300 years old or dating from about 1300 B.C.

Other pottery shards found in Fiji, at Ba, Sigatoka and in Lakeba dated back to 1500 B.C. or 3500 B.P. This earliest potter has the same detailed designs as those found in shards of the same period in Samoa, Tonga and New Caledonia. Lapita pottery was first discovered at a site in New Caledonia called Lapita, hence its present name. It might just as well have been found on Fiji, Tonga or Samoa first and given another name, but the name Lapita has stuck. Since these early voyages probably came from the west, Fiji or New Caledonia would probably have been reached first.

At the lowest level of his digs, Best found an abundance of bird skeletons, indicating, he feels, the early arrival of man on the islands. Fiji's many birds would have had little fear of man upon his arrival at the islands and were more easily hunted and caught. Higher up in the soil of his digs was evidence of cannibalism: human bones that had been crushed, burned and chewed. Other bones showed that the early people had domesticated chickens with them and the carbonized seeds from the cooking fires showed that more than 20 kinds of fruits were available to them, some probably brought from South East Asia or elsewhere.

Best also found pearl shell fish hooks, those often found in Polynesia but not in Melanesia. These are the only such hooks found outside of Polynesia, further lending evidence that Fiji was part of early Polynesia. A flake of obsidian was also found at the dig. The sharp volcanic glass can only be found at a few special locations in the Pacific such as Tonga, Vanuatu or the Manu'a Island group in far eastern Samoa. Best theorized that the obsidian had come from Vanuatu or Tonga, and it was clear evidence that these early Lapita People moved freely from island to island and must have been good navigators with large ships.

Curiously, thought Best, the earliest settled site in Lakeba was found against the side of a cliff, right on the flat coast line. It would have been a difficult place to defend, unlike the hill-top fortified villages that were to follow. One of these hill-top forts was less than one mile away. This fortified village in Ulunikoro, high up on the ridges of a rocky hill. Best says that it was populated 200 years later than the village site on the coast below it.

Best believes the Ulunikoro site to be the largest fortified village in Fiji and perhaps the largest in the entire South Pacific. Ulunikoro had miles of man-made terraces for its agricultural tenants. It had "massive defenses" which were stone walls laboriously built and guarded by surveillance points reaching out at intervals beyond the walls. it had deep pits from which it appears people may have been hurled into the depths. The skeletal remains of people, anyway, were found at the bottom

Simon Best with a piece of Lapita pottery.

of the deep pits. The village was apparently abandoned about 700 years ago.

Who were these people building such a massive fortification and against whom were they fortifying their city? It is a mystery to Best and other archaeologists. Sadly, many of the ancient walls from the mysterious city of Ulunikoro have had their stones removed by the local Public Works Department to use in the construction of Lakeba's airfield, Tubou's jetty and other local building projects.

It is now thought that the arrival of Lutunasobasoba at Vuda was a more recent arrival of Fijians. Vuda, a few miles from Viseisei village, rises 350 feet above the bank of a small river. Its vertical stone face provides ample protection for 25 house platforms, the mounds still visible above the undergrowth. The uppermost five are supposedly the burekalou, the priests quarters and the house of Lutunasobasoba himself.

Legend says that Lutunasobasoba reached the shores near what is now Viseisei and chose Vuda for his "yavutu," or capital. Though it is a small, steep peak, it still had four major temples on its summit, erected to the gods Erovunavuda, Vunayawa, Leka and Lutunasobasoba. The nearby villagers still claim that they are the descendants of Lutunasobasoba, or the Kai Vuda.

The British archaeologist Gifford began excavations at Vuda in 1947. Gifford wrote of the "stone-faced platform crowns the central crag, rising as an acropolis." Gifford had a high respect for Fijian traditions and understood the grandeur of Fiji's past, so he left a traditional gift of kava (yaqona) at Lutunasobasoba's temple before, and after, his dig.

Gifford took time to classify 69 species of mollusk shells found into he ashes of the cooking fires and carbon-dated the earliest artifacts that he could uncover from the site. His earliest date was a surprisingly young 650 years before present (BP) or only about 1255 to 1305 A.D. This would make Lutunasobasoba

TAKIVELEYAWA.

The hilltop fortress of Takiveleyawa.

and his Kanitoni canoes relative newcomers to Fiji. By his theories, Lutunasobasoba and the Lapita people were not the same people.

Perhaps it was Lutunasobasoba and his Kanitoni canoes that forced out the earlier Polynesian/ Lapita people? Was Fiji and Ulunikoro the ancient capital of Polynesia? With the invasion of Melanesian's led by Lutunasobasoba the Polynesians pulled back to

BURE OF NA TAVASARA, TAVIUNI.

their mighty naval base at Tongatapu. For 650 years the Tongans and Fijians then fought over control of the eastern Fijian islands of Lau. The Polynesians maintained control however of such northern islands as Rotuma and Kapingamaringi.

Ancient Stone Inscriptions in Fiji

Unlike Tonga, Fiji has stone inscriptions that continue to baffle archaeologists today. According to Kim Gravelle in *Fiji's Times* rock drawings have been found in almost all of Fiji's major islands. "Yet," says Gravelle, "villagers treat the mysterious works with indifference, calling them simply *na vatu vola*...the inscribed rocks. They've always been there, villagers shrug. There is no superstition and no reverence toward them: certainly they are not *tabu*."

Some of the rock inscriptions take the form of concentric circles, usually three or more circles inside each other. This same motif is found etched in stone in New Caledonia, Vanuatu, Papua New Guinea, New Zealand, Tonga, Hawaii and the Marquesas islands, to name just a few. Generally it is thought that such petroglyphs are meant to represent the sun and the moon.

Other petroglyphs are apparently glyphs of a written language, though usually in a jumbled order. One of the best examples of

PRIEST'S BOWL.

A Fijian priest's ceremonial bowl.

some sort of petroglyph script is near Dakuniba in the southeast corner of Vanua Levu. Extremely hard stone tools (such as basalt) were used at Dakuniba a pattern of geometric shapes into a number of large flat rocks. In a straight line parallel with the sea, two other boulders are simi-

Cakabau in traditional turban.

larly marked, and there are indentations nearby where stone tools have been sharpened. Certain letters may be discerned that look similar to Phoenician, Hebrew, Demotic Egyptian script and the mysterious Minoan-Hittite scripts such as the Phaistos Disc found in Crete.

Doric Greek, ancient Hittite (which had a hieroglyphic script and a character script) the strange Rongo Rongo script of Rapa Nui were all written in the Boustrophedon pattern of "as the ox plows." This unusual pattern of writing right to left and then the next line left to right and so on, was used by the Pacific's only known written language, Rongo Rongo writing. These unusual scripts are seemingly all connected and therefore cast a certain light on to the mysteries of the Pacific.

Says Kim Gravelle of the Dakuniba inscriptions, "If the strange markings are a written language, it is a language without any apparent form, since the characters are randomly spaced and not in any line. But there is one good reason why they can't be easily dismissed as haphazard scribbling: more than 150 miles away, in a cave reached only by an underwater entrance, another series of engravings exists which is startlingly similar. Cut into the limestone walls of Yasawa-i-Lau cave in the Yasawas, these

A Fijian temple-pyramid, the Buke of Na Ututu.

petroglyphs embellish five neat, round steps which form a ladder to a shelf in the cave."

It has been suggested that the shelf was a throne for an early priest or for a stone idol. Copies of the Dakuniba and Yasawa-i-Lau petroglyhs were sent to the British Museum in 1937, the experts of the time said they could see no relationships between any known ancient or modern scripts and

SACRED STONES.

suggested that they were magical symbols. However, our knowledge of ancient scripts has grown since that time and we may be able to trace the script back to India or the Middle East.

It is also curious that the cave with the inscriptions at Yasawa-i-Lau is now underwater. At the time that the inscriptions were made, possibly 3500 years ago, the water level around Fiji may have changed quite a bit. The cave may not have been underwater at that time, as sea levels have been shown to have changed drastically during this period (see appendix).

Other rock engravings in Fiji are mentioned in the 1883 book *Camping Amongst Cannibals* which describes a trip into the Sigatoka Valley. The author writes that near a village called Tawalika "...there the limestone walls have been decorated... with representations of canoes and men, and other objects, the nature of which we could

not make out. They have chipped the designs with a stone in a series of dots on the side of the cave, and have then filled in the little cavities with a light coloured clay..."[17]

On the small island of Vatulele, south of Viti Levu, are cliff-side rock paintings above a beach on the western side of the island. The badly weathered paintings depict birds, faces, a large canoe with sails and steering oar, a hand, a cross on a shield and other motifs. One of the birds is easily identified at a jungle fowl known as 'mangu hegwa,' in the Vatulele dialect, which is a descendant of domesticated fowl brought to Fiji

Children play near baki stones. Note the tall standing stone and a broken stone in the foreground.

about 3000 years ago.

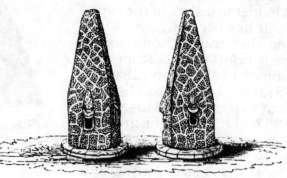

Fijian oracle chambers as drawn in 1845.

Other rock inscriptions in Fiji have been compared to those in other parts of the Pacific. "In Hawaii, there is a field of flat stones, their surfaces carved with a tapestry of concentric circles and straight, dotted lines. At Vuinadi in Vanua Levu, a boulder has been inscribed with markings so similar it is difficult to avoid reaching any 'linking' conclusions. But much more research will be necessary before such conclusions are possible." states Kim Gravelle.[17]

FEEJEE ORACLE.

Other similar spiral and concentric circle petroglyphs were noted by Oxford scholar John Macmillan Brown in the southern most parts of Vanuatu and at Kawhia in the northwest part of the north island of New Zealand. Spirals like this are found all over the world including such ancient megalithic sites as Tarxien in Malta and Newgrange in Ireland.

Standing Stones and Baki Rites

Rounded standing stones in ancient Fiji were part of the religion and ceremonial worship. Tall rounded stones, often with spirals or

Dillion's Rock with a Fijian canoe.

concentric circles on them, were once anointed with kava (yaqona) and rock walls marked the boundaries of open-air temples used in the secretive 'Baki' rites. These ancient fertility rites were held annually and the ceremony was so secret that the punishment was death for revealing what went on.

Baki ceremonies were thought to have originated in western Viti Levu. The secret rites were held annually and were to insure continued fertility for both crops and people. *Yabaki* means year in Fijian. The ceremonies were held in walled 'naga' or 'nanaga' sites which were cleared areas hidden deep in the interior of the islands. It was rumored that the rites included sorcery and orgiastic sex.

Since the betrayal of the rites could result in death information on the 'baki' rites was scant until 1909 when an account of the rites was written by Ratu Savenaca Duratalo of Navosa, Colo West, broke the tabu. In his report, he said that the rites originated at Vuda and Nadi, and that there were four baki divisions, *Rukuruku, Visina, Saqere* and *Buca. Nanaga* sites were cleared and weeded until they resembled a village *rara*, and stones were placed around the clearing, one for every youth initiated into the sect. Usually, the *naga* were hidden in the midst of sacred *ivi trees.*

Ratu Savenaca said youths initially spent only three days at the site, speaking in hushed tones, learning from the elders. On the third day, they were sent back to their villages for one year "to plant yams and fatten pigs." When they reentered the naga, this time for 14 days and nights, their heads and beards were shaved and their bodies smeared with burnt ash of candle nuts.

Ratu Savenaca, probably fearing death, describes very little of what actually happened inside the walls of the naga enclosure but the rites were said to be connected to circumcision, warfare training, and teaching social and sexual tabus.

The Fijian chief Vendovi wearing a traditional turban.

A detailed description of one initiation ceremony inside a naga enclosure was made by historian Basil Thomson, say Kim Gravelle. Thomson wrote that initiates were made to approach the site on hands and knees, the eerie booming of a bamboo trumpet submerged in water adding to the spookiness of the scene.

Says Thomson,"As the participant entered the naga a dreadful sight appalled them. Right across the entrance lay the naked body of a dead man, smeared with black paint... Above him lay another body and under this hideous arch they were made to crawl... At a cry from the elder in charge of the ceremony, the 'dead men' suddenly rose up... and ran to wash off the blood... of pigs."

Women were supposedly forbidden to come near the naga sites, although it appears that women were sometimes allowed inside the enclosure, probably for "manhood training purposes" and the alleged orgiastic rites. Stone altars inside the naga were repeatedly bathed with kava and a secret potion was said to be held in the special baki pots that supposedly made the initiates insensible to pain.

Today, the stone fences and tall naga standing stones still exist in Viti Levu, near the upper reaches of the Wainimala, Sigatoka, and Navua rivers. Baki rites continued well into the 19th century, ending eventually with the eventual adoption of Christianity.

Curiously, the anointing of rounded standing stones in Fiji is identical to the Hindu practice of anointing a lingam stone. In Hindu India, today as in ancient times, rounded standing stones, probably meant to represent an erect penis, are anointed with clarified butter and worshipped as part of the Hindu fertility rites. This identical practice in Fiji lends further credence to a Hindu-Indian-origin for the Polynesians and to the supposition that Fiji was once a major Polynesian island group.

In his book *Hindu America?*,[20] (1960) Chaman Lal argues that the ancient Hindus were crossing the Pacific to Mexico and California as early as 1000 B.C. if not before. Lal argues convincingly that the ancient Chinese were making voyages to Mexico as early as 2500 B.C. and that when the Chinese state of the Emperor Wu fell in 473 B.C. the Hindus became the main

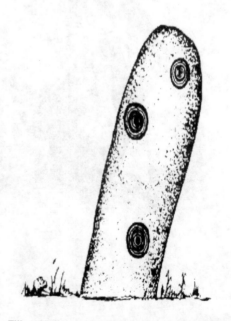

Fijian standing stone with concentric circles used in Baki rites, as drawn in 1860.

voyagers across the Pacific in the lucrative trade in jade, gold, magic mushrooms and herbal longevity potions favored by the Chinese. Jade could be also be obtained from a Polynesian source: New Zealand.[20]

Says Chaman Lal in *Hindu America?*, "Those who believe that the ancient peoples of Asia were incapable of crossing the ocean have completely lost sight of what the literary sources tell us concerning their ships and their navigation. The kings of Wu undertook military expeditions against distant islands, perhaps Formosa or the Ryukyu Archipelago, and from one of them brought back thousands of prisoners of war. This presupposes, of course, the existences of large ocean going ships. Since the State of Wu was annihilated in 473 B.C. these expeditions must have occurred before that date. In the first century A.D. the periplus of the Erythraean Sea mentions the large ships of southern India which engaged in trade with the countries of the East. A Chinese source of the third century A.D. describes vessels from southern Asia which were 150 feet in length, had four masts and were able to carry six to seven hundred men and one thousand metric tons of merchandise. When the Buddhist pilgrim Fahien returned from Ceylon to China, in 414 A.D., the ship on which he embarked carried two hundred persons. It did not sail along the coasts, but right across the ocean. In 817 A.D., a Chinese author speaks of the large ships of southern Asia which could carry a thousand men and whose crews consisted largely of Malayans. There seems to be no reason why these Asiatic vessels could not have crossed the Pacific Ocean just as well as Magellan did later with his much smaller ships."

Indeed, the gigantic trading ships of the ancient Chinese, Hindus, Phoenicians and Egyptians were larger than ships of Columbus, Magellan, and Cook. Captain William Bligh of the famous Bounty mutiny was cast adrift with a few men in waters off western Tonga in 1789 and made it all the way to Timor in Indonesia in an open boat with nothing more than a simple sail and oars, still the

Queen Rewa of Fiji.

longest voyage in an open boat on record. As Bligh passed between the two major islands of Fiji, Vanua Levu and Viti Levu, he was pursued by several large Fijian canoes, all swifter and larger than his small craft. Fortunately a sudden thunder squall occurred and Bligh was able to escape as it became dark.

The Pyramids of Rotuma

The northern Polynesian island of Rotuma has Fiji's most mysterious megalithic site. It is on the remote island of Rotuma, still part of the Fiji islands but laying far north of the others. In a brief article in the *Royal Anthropological Institute Journal* in 1876 (no. 6, pp 5-6) the author W.W. Wood speaks about the massive stone blocks:

"On reading Lieutenant Oliver's paper on 'The Megalithic Structures of the Channel Islands,' I bethought me of some notes and sketches made years ago on the Island of Rotumah, in the South Pacific Ocean, where I met with some curious stone tombs, composed of masses so large that it was difficult to conceive the means by which the natives had been able to move and arrange them. The Island of Rotumah is an outlier of the Fiji group, though at a considerable distance to the north. The natives are of a different race and lighter colour than those of the Fiji's, and are distinguished (or were) for their amiable and inoffensive manners. The island is a small one, and not very high, except towards one end, where there is a precipice overlooking the sea, with a large flat terrace at its base, overflowed at high tide.

"The megalithic monuments on the principle island were not far from the beach, near some very fine old trees. The tombs consisted of a low platform of earth, enclosed by slabs of stone set vertically, and in

Fijian musical instruments such as log drums and pan pipes. Pan pipes were commonly used in ancient Greece and Peru.

the centre one or more huge stones of irregular shape—mere masses of rock—some of which must weigh many tons. The natives seemed shy of giving any information respecting these curious structures, and from a European, who had settled on the island, we could only learn that they were tombs. The remarkable point was that these simple people should, without the aid of machinery, have been able to raise and arrange these great masses of rock."[25]

The giant pyramid-tombs of Rotuma are no doubt connected with the similar structures in Tonga and elsewhere. Indeed, it shows how Rotuma, the last Polynesian stronghold in Fiji was the most important island of all. It was important because it was a major naval base for the Tongan-Lapita-Polynesians on the northwest edge of the realm. The early Lapita-Polynesians coming from Indonesia were sailing to the north and south of New Guinea along the equator into the western Pacific. The Melanesian islands of New Britain, New Ireland and the Solomon's were already inhabited by Melanesian's who had apparently been in New Guinea and New Ireland at least 40,000 years.

They continued into the western Pacific island groups of New Caledonia, Vanuatu, Fiji, Tonga and Samoa. Rotuma was an isolated but important island on the northern route into the Central Pacific. Once a ship had made it from eastern Indonesia past the inhospitable islands of New Guinea and the Solomons the ship's first major land fall would be Rotuma, a small island with megalithic pyramids and other structures. The next major stop would be the sheltered lagoon at Tongatapu and the city of Mu'a.

Indeed, the pyramid structures at Rotuma help us shed light on the antiquity of the langi-pyramids at Mu'a. The pyramids at Rotuma and those at Mu'a must have been built at the same time: probably around 1500 B.C.

There is a great deal of other evidence that the Polynesians once controlled much of Melanesia, with island bases in New Hanover Island (north of New Ireland, part of Papua New Guinea), Rennel Island, Vanuatu, New Caledonia and Fiji. Over time the Melanesian races moved eastward and conquered the Pacific Islands of New Britain, New Ireland, New Hanover, the Solomons, Vanuatu, New Caledonia and finally Fiji. Fijians and Tongans were still fighting over the eastern Lau Group

Fijian pottery as drawn in 1858. Note the double and triple pots. Such unusual pots are common in coastal Peru.

A giant double-canoe used in Papua New Guinea.

of Fiji at the time of European exploration. Some islands, like Rennell, Rotuma and Kapingamaringi atoll, today part of Micronesia, are still Polynesian in population.

Evidence of these voyages can be found in the standing stones and other ancient structures found on certain islands of Melanesia. Very tall standing stones can be found in New Guinea and others can be found in New Britain, New Hanover, and other sites.

The New Guinea island of New Hanover is well situated for a Polynesian naval base that could arrive from the west and then continue out into the western Pacific. Says the former British New Guinea range officer Keith Willey in his 1965 book *Assignment New Guinea*[80] while speaking of a German plantation owner: "Natives on New Hanover still spoke with respect of the 'men belong time before', he said. He believed these were a race with a superior culture who had disappeared generations ago. 'Either they migrated elsewhere in canoes, or they may have been wiped out in an epidemic; perhaps by malaria, which destroyed the Maya civilization in Central America,' he said."

New Hanover is said to have a number of lost structures, including pyramids, rock inscriptions and other ancient works. Says Keith Willey, "On the slopes of The Mother (a mountain peak) he had found a number of basalt obelisks, apparently of volcanic origin, which he believed could provide a link with temples built by sun worshipers in Europe, Egypt, Central and South America, and other widely scattered areas. He had seen similar ruins in Germany where people were sacrificed every spring, centuries ago; and believed the New Hanover discovery could be a clue to some early form of humanity which had spread throughout the world. the obelisks, huge, domed boulders, long as a normal room and half as high, were carved with the faces of birds, outlines of fish, and lines and whorls, all pointing east at the rising sun. One had an altar, perhaps for human sacrifice; with runnels where the blood could pour out onto the ground."[80]

Other curious stone remains on other Melanesian islands are mentioned by Willey, "The Director of Native Affairs J.K. McCarthy, said that on Tingwon Island, twenty miles west of New Hanover, the natives told legends of a strange people who had visited them centuries before, then sailed away and perished at sea. Their bodies were resurrected and returned to existence as upright stones. Such relics had been found in the area, including one carved like a wheel, although the wheel was unknown there. Another legend told of a cave in the mountains of New Hanover where the strangers had stored huge amounts of cargo before going off in their canoes.

"Jack West of Lae, who has lived in New Guinea since the early 1920s, said that in 1946 he found carved boulders on an island off the coast of New Britain. A very old obelisk seven or eight feet high faced the rising sun, while surrounding it were smaller stones, half-buried, and carved with primitive designs. The setting was similar to another group of stones he had seen on an island of the Schouten Group, off Wewak, when he was there many years before as a labour recruiter.

"A Rabaul expert speculated that the temple on New Hanover may be linked with the Ingiat cult which is centred in the Duke of York Islands, east of Rabaul, but has adherents among the Tolais of New Britain.

"Ingiat priests claim the ability to turn into fish, birds, or reptiles; and to work spells that can kill from a distance.

"On New Ireland itself I met a planter, Peter Murray,

This Rennel Islander lives in Melanesia but is actually a Polynesian. From Peter Buck.

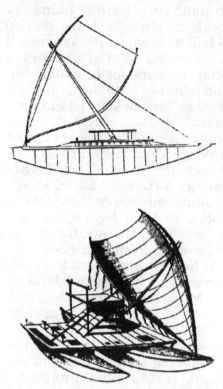

A Fijian double-canoe.

who had found a ring of boulders 'like Stonehenge,' on Unea, main island of the Vitu group, about eighty miles north-west of the New Britain post of Talasea. He said: 'The stones are rectangular, each about eleven feet long, and carved with circles and squiggly lines like hieroglyphics. Two old men, Uva and Umbelevi, guided me to where they are positioned on top of a 2,500 foot peak known as Kambu. The stones are not volcanic; obviously they have been quarried elsewhere and taken up the mountain by some means. They are so ancient that the natives do not even have legends about them.'"[80]

Apparently, the ancient Polynesians and Fijians came from Indonesia, largely by-passed mainland New Guinea, and maintained island supply bases at such places as Rotuma and the Trobriand islands in the Torres Straits of southern New Guinea. From these island bases the ships went on to inner Pacific island groups that included Fiji, Tonga and Samoa.

Fijian Firewalking

The tradition of Fijian firewalking began on the island of Mbengga, which is directly south of Viti Levu, the main island. Even today, the only Fijians who are able to do firewalking are from this island. In fact, the only firewalkers are from a single 'matangali', or extended family, from that island.

The Fijians from Mbengga prepare a very large 'lovo', or underground oven, which is perhaps 12 feet in diameter. This oven is simply a dug out depression in the earth and is about 18 inches deep. This is then mostly filled with large, gray river stones which appear to be like basalt. These stones are about the size of a breadbox or typewriter. A raging bonfire is then built on top of the stones. As the bonfire dies down, the stones are white-hot, sizzling, and surrounded by glowing coals. It is then that the Fijians walk, slowly and deliberately, on the stones!

Legend has it that the ability to walk on fire was first given to a Mbengga warrior named Tui-na-vinggalita who spared the life of a spirit god he had caught while fishing for eels. Today the descendants of Tui-na-vinggalita act as *mbete* (high priest) of the firewalkers and only members of his tribe, the Sawau, perform the ceremony. Firewalkers are not permitted to have contact with women or eat any coconut for two weeks prior to a firewalk.

Firewalking was common in ancient India, where it also spread to Bali and probably other islands of Indonesia. Firewalking was also known in Hawaii and it may have practiced in many areas of prehistory, including Tonga and Samoa in the past. Firewalking is still practiced in parts of India today, and has recently had a revival in the United States.

Other areas that practiced firewalking may be submerged. A curious report of land animals preserved in a prehistoric cave in Fiji appeared in the New Zealand *Herald* on May 31, 1990. In a story entitled "Monsters found in the Fiji Deep" by Geoff Spencer a professional diver from Sydney named K. Deacon was quoted as saying he discovered several land animals in a marine cave 51.5 kilometers from one of Fiji's resort islands (he does not say which).

The cave is now part of a reef about 50 meters underwater. He believes that the cave must have once been above sea level: "We have found what appears to be two adults, one adolescent and one juvenile. They bear no resemblance to any marine creature I know. The adult skulls were about one meter long with a total body length of eight to ten meters. They look prehistoric and perhaps were land animals or an amphibious species."

A Fijian canoe with D'Urville's ship *L'Astrolab* in 1833.

Cannibalism and the Tongan Influence in Fiji

Cannibalism and continual warfare played an important part in the history of the islands for hundreds, if not thousands, of years. Long known as the Cannibal Islands, the Fijian feudal native aristocracy practiced customs which would today seem cruel, callous, and barbarous. In this tyrannical, medieval society people were buried alive under the posts of new houses, war canoes were launched over the bodies of young girls, and widows of chiefs were strangled to keep their masters company in the spirit world.

Prisoners were baked whole in ovens, and it was forbidden to touch the flesh. Instead, special forks were used. The Fijians called human flesh "puaka mbalavu" or "long pig." It is generally remarked that human flesh tastes a great deal like pork.

In 1789, after the *Bounty* mutiny, Capt. Bligh was chased by canoe-loads of hostile cannibals as he and his crew rowed between the two main islands of Fiji on their way to Portuguese Timor. The sea between Vitu Levu and Tasawas is still known as Bligh Water. Even though they had been rowing for many weeks, and were hungry and thirsty, Bligh and his men were able to outdistance the pursuing natives, perhaps out of their fear of a fate worse than death. Bligh's careful observations gave Europeans, for the first time, an accurate picture of Fiji.

Most Polynesian historians believe that Fiji and Tonga were closely related in the past, but became more and more separate as time went on. Tonga remained in control of most of the eastern Lau group right up until the time of European colonization. In 1847, Ma'afu, a cousin of the Tu'i Tonga and a Tongan in search of "overseas adventure", came to the Lau group of Fiji as a sea-going warlord of sorts. Many Tongans already lived in the Lau group and raiding of various islands occurred regularly among Tongans and Fijians.

Fijian log drummer.

Mafioso "good works" came to the attention of the Tui Tonga and in 1853 Ma'afu became the governor of all Tongans in the Lau group, as well as the defacto representative of the Tongan Wesleyan church. Ma'afu was later instrumental in the Christian conversion of Fiji's recognized head chief Cakobau to Wesleyan Christianity. In 1853 Cakobau allowed the first Wesleyan missionary to live in the trading town of Bau and a year later the king of Tonga sent a message to Cakobau to convert and enjoy the support of Tonga or Tonga would invade Fiji, its former domain anyway. Cakobau wisely converted to Christianity, thereby avoiding the Tongan invasion.

A Fijian clown drawn in 1845.

The forced conversion of Cakobau by the king of Tonga is evidence that Fiji was the western extension of Tonga's far-flung Pacific empire that included Hawaii, Tahiti, Easter Island and New Zealand. Fiji was invaded by Melanesian's from the west and slowly lapsed in chaos. Tonga lost its control of the western islands and the main islands of Viti Levu and Vanua Levu but maintained control of the eastern islands closer to Tonga. The new Fiji fell into savage cannibal warfare that had afflicted New Guinea for tens of thousands of years. Without a strong central government like Tonga, Fiji fell into a chaotic localized state of war that lasted for hundred of years.

When Fiji was first discovered by European explorers the main islands lacked any powerful chiefs and villages raided each other in a continual orgy of violence and cannibalism. This sorry state of social life in Fiji was something that had occurred relatively recently and it seems certain that the island had a central government in the ancient past, possibly centered at Ulunikoro.

It is interesting to view ancient Fiji in the light of a vast Pacific empire centered on the lagoon at Tongatapu. From the large, sheltered lagoon the great double canoes left in all directions to the many islands of Polynesia. They went south to New Zealand, west to Tahiti, Rapa Iti and Rapa Nui, north to Samoa, Kiribati and Hawaii and west to Fiji, Rotuma and Vanuatu. It was to the west as well that the main trading bases were located: Bali, Sumatra, Cambodia and India.

Indeed, one the ancient races of Southeast Asia is the Nagas, a seafaring race of people who traded in their "Serpent Boats" similar to the Dragon ships of the Vikings. The Nagas are associated with ancient India and are credited with building Angor Wat in Cambodia and spreading Hinduism throughout Indonesia, perhaps even out into the Pacific. The popular tourist resort island of Bali is the last remnant of this ancient empire which once stretched from southern India to Tonga and beyond.

Solomon Islander.

Fijian Princesses.

Fijian Breadfruit Carrier.

Native Girls Dressed for a Meke.

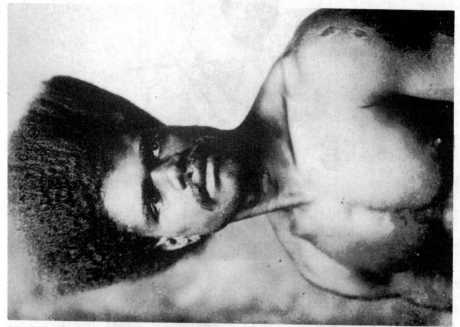

Two Fijian chiefs in photos from the early 1900s. Their appearance may be part Tongan.

Fossilised Rock.

Highest Fijian Dwelling on Kadavu.

Upper Navua River.

A Fijian Warrior.

Top: Fijian warriors demonstrate various spears and weapons for an early photographer. Bottom: Fijians reenact a cannibal feast for another photograph.

Top: Fijian canoes in Suva harbor circa 1910. Bottom: Sailmaking in a beach village.

Some of the Leading Chiefs of Fiji.

CHAPTER 4

SAMOA &
THE SEARCH FOR HAVAI'IKI

We came from Hawaiki-the-Great
From Hawaiki-the-long, from Havaiki-the-Distant.
—Maori Legend quoted by Peter Buck
in *Vikings of the Pacific*

Samoa is a group of islands that could rightfully be called the heart of Polynesia. It is generally thought that Samoa was settled at about the same time as Tonga, circa 1200 B.C. by the Lapita People. The oldest known site of human occupation in Samoa discovered so far is Mulifanua in the district of A'ana on Upolu. This site was discovered in the mid-1970s by archaeologists from the University of Utah. A carbon-14 date of approximately 1000 B.C. was obtained, placing Mulifanua in the time-frame as Lapita sites in New Caledonia, Fiji, Vanuatu and Tonga.

The site at Mulifanua was determined to be an old village site which was now almost completely covered by water and was at the bottom of a lagoon, indicating that ocean levels had changed or some subsidence of the Samoan islands had taken place (or both).

Other ancient Lapita sites were discovered by the University of Utah at Manono and near Fasito'otai. These sites were assigned dates by the University of 2,600 B.P. and 1,850 B.P. respectively. Two other ancient sites with Lapita associated remains are Sasoa'a in Flefa Valley of Upolu and Vailele near Apia. Vailele was determined to have been occupied by at least 300 B.C.[29]

The Great Pyramid of Samoa

Samoa contains a number of large stone structures, including what is said to be the largest pyramid structure in the South Pacific, the Pulemelei mound at Palauli in southeastern Savai'i. The structures do not contain the large quarried stone blocks associated with Tonga, Rapa Nui or the Marquesas however.

Samoa has several large pyramidal structures such as Pulemelei and Laupule, plus star mounds such as at Mulifanua, Upolu or Vaito'omuli on the island of Savai'i. Other stoneworks of ancient construction include pathways, agricultural terraces, walls and forts. These extensive stone remains are indicative of Samoa's organized society in ancient times.

John MacMillan Brown, former Chancellor of the University of New Zealand, had this to say about Samoan pyramids in his book, *The Riddle of the Pacific*,[1] "In the south of Upolu of the Samoan group, Mr. Edgar N. Heycock has just found numerous truncated and stepped pyramids of stone ranging from ten to thirty feet in height, twenty to sixty feet in width and ninety to two hundred feet in length; and from these there are traces of paved ways down to the sea. Farther to east and not far from the Equator, Malden Island... is covered with truncated pyramids of coral blocks capped with dolmens and approached by paved ways from the sea."

Curiously, the Samoans seem to lost all knowledge of the origins or use of these pyramids and star-mounds. Says the Samoan historian Malama Meleisea in *Lagaga: A Short History of Western Samoa*,[29] "There are many mysteries about Samoa's prehistoric past. There are no stories which explain the function of the many great earth and stone monuments, such as Pulemelei... Some of these great mounds have

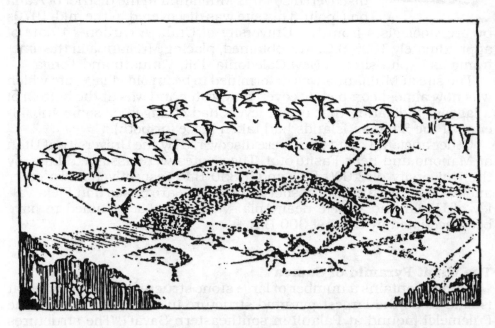

The Great Pyramid of Samoa, the Pulemelei mound at Palauli, Savai'i.

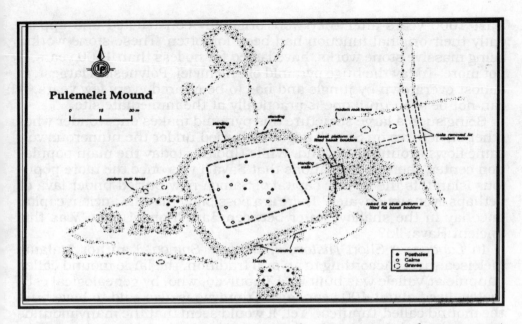

Pulemelei Mound

been investigated by archaeologists and one ten-pointed monument at Mulifanua has been associated with a C14 date of 1,595 years ago."

Samoan's seem to have forgotten the purpose of pyramids and star mounds, which have all fallen into disuse. While pyramid-mounds exist on many islands of the Pacific, from Tonga to the Marquesas, from Hawai'i to Tahiti and Rapa Nui, their use is usually said to be of ceremonial nature or, in the case of Tonga, as burial mounds. In Samoa, the mounds are generally attributed to the former royal amusement of "pigeon hunting."

"It is difficult to accept the popular explanation that the mounds were built for snaring pigeons, because of the great amount of labour and organization which was involved in their construction. The ten-pointed 'star mound' at Mulifanua was partially excavated by the Utah University team in 1974 and 1976. No post holes or burial remains were found in it, which suggests that the star mounds were not house platforms or graves. This mound has a walled path leading from it to a large clearing which was probably a malae. Walled paths have been found in association with similar monuments in other areas. One theory is that the mounds were built for religious reasons and served as temples or places of worship." says Malama Meleisea.[29]

While pigeon hunting may have been a popular sport for the privileged class of Samoa, it seems doubtful that these huge earthworks were constructed just for catching pigeons. It may well be that later kings of Samoa and Tonga did go on holiday jaunts to these mounds and catch pigeons, but it would seem that this sport took place at least 1000 years after they were originally constructed and apparently their original function had been forgotten. These stone works, being massive stone works, have lasted for no less than 1500 years, if not more. Today the huge pyramid of Pulemelei, Polynesia's largest, is almost overgrown by jungle and has to be cleared every few years. It can not be seen until one is practically at the immediate site.

Being such a large structure this pyramid makes one wonder what other structures on Savai'i might be buried under the numerous volcanic flows around the island. While Upolu is today the main population center, there is indications that Savai'i was once the more populous island. Is the former capital of Samoa now buried under lava or perhaps even underwater? There is a possibility that the ancient capital once lay in the shallow water between Savai'i and Upolu. Was this ancient Havai'iki?

In *Lagaga: A Short History of Western Samoa*,[29] author Malama Meleisea says, "According to an oral tradition, the large mound called Laupule at Vailele was built by a Tupuivao, who, by genealogical estimates, lived about 400 years ago. Tupuivao is also said to have built the mound called Taputea." Yet, it would seem that the many mounds on Samoa have a much older date, including the large mound at Vailele. Therefore, it would seem that the oral genealogical tables are in error

Early excavation of the Pulemelei mound.

by over a thousand years.

This would only be logical over long periods of time where written records were not kept. Recent kings and families would be more accurate but as the oral historian went further back in time the names of kings would actually be of Family dynasties that lasted several hundred years, as many dynasties do. Therefore, similar to Egyptian, Hittite, Persian and other kings, the Samoan and Tongan kings of antiquity would have had the same name for a number of generations. Similarly, the Toltecs kings of northern Mexico nearly all had the name of Quetzalcoatl.

In a similar way we can also see how the genealogical list of the kings of Tonga may also be incorrect as theorized earlier. The list of Tongan kings, in theory, should go back to at least 1000 B.C. Surely the Tongan kingship did not begin 500 years ago as some historians now contend. Both of these lists should be considered carefully as dynastic documents concerning a series of rulers, often with the same names. Malama Meleisea is absolutely correct in the suggestion that the Samoan table should go back in time to building the building of the pyramids on the island, i.e. 1595 B.P.

The star mound at Vaito'omuli, Savai'i.

The Search For Havai'iki

Havai'iki was said to be the Polynesian homeland and some scholars have noted the linguistic similarity between Samoa's largest island, Savai'i and Havai'iki. The far northern islands of Hawai'i are the closest, linguistically, to the legendary Polynesian homeland of Hawai'iki. However, they are considered too far away from the rest of the world to have been the legendary homeland of Polynesians. Historians generally believe that the Hawaiian islands were settled last by the Polynesians, not first.

Many Samoans believe that Savai'i was ancient Havai'iki, the original homeland or ancient capital of Polynesia, now a forgotten backwater of Polynesia. Savai'i is the largest island of the Samoan group but the many volcanic eruptions on the island and the various devastating cyclones have taken their toll on the island. Even in recent years this has been a problem. The Mount Matavanu eruptions of 1905 to 1911 created a moonscape of the northeastern part of Savai'i and covered many villages in flows of lava from 10 meters to 150 meters in thickness. In February of 1990 and December of 1991 the cyclones 'Ofa and Val devastated the northwest corner of the Savai'i, utterly destroying the villages in the area, including an ancient starmound.

The location of Havaiiki was believed by early Polynesian historian Peter S. Buck as Raiatea, the central island in the Society Islands.

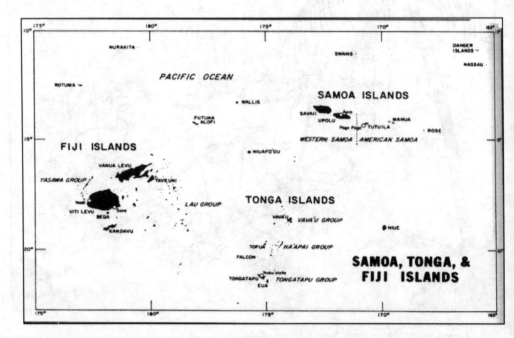

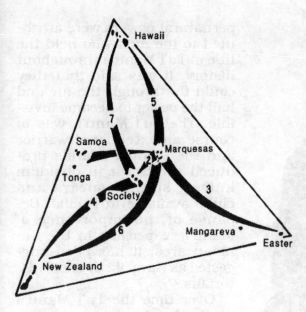

James Michener makes the same claim in his epic historical book *Hawaii*. Other suggestions for Havai'iki have been Rarotonga and the Samoan island of Manu'a. Tongatapu was probably the early capital of Polynesia and may have been Havai'iki. It is also quite possible that Havai'iki was another land in East Asia, India or even Egypt and Middle East where the Polynesians originally came from. Others have suggested ancient Peru or even a sunken continent with a capital city near to present day Hawaii. Though concepts of a sunken Pacific continent do not find much favor with orthodox science, there is ample evidence of drastic changes in the land-sea relationship in the Pacific and of underwater ruins and other submerged areas formerly occupied by humans (the Lapita site at Mulifanua for example, or the underwater structures on Pohnpei in Micronesia). The Pacific Rim, known as the Ring of Fire, is the most active tectonic plate of Earth's geological zones.

Manu'a, Sacred Islands of the Gods

According to Samoan tradition the small eastern island archipelago of Manu'a is the first creation of land, the first land to emerge at the hands of the god Tagaloa. The Manu'a group consists of three small islands, Ofu, Olosega and Ta'u. These islands are all of a volcanic nature being a complex of volcanic cones that have been buried by lava from two merging "shield flows." During a long period of dormancy and heavy rainfall deep valleys have been carved out, leaving cliffs from 90 meters high to 365 meters high around the coasts of the three islands. Ta'u Island is a volcanic crater with half of it fallen away, leaving a spectacular circular cliffs and volcanic spire. All the islands abound with volcanic rock and even obsidian, a valued trade item. Obsidian blades are actually sharper than metal blades, but are easily fractured.

Perhaps because of the obsidian trade the Tu'i Manu'a was considered the "Sovereign of Polynesia" by many Polynesian historians. Su-

Somoan orator Lauati Namulauulu (died 1914).

pernatural powers were attributed to the men who held the title of Tu'i Manu'a throughout history. It was said that they could fly through the air and had the power to become invisible. The Tu'i Manu'a was of course an exceptional warrior and the Manu'a Islands produced the finest in obsidian knives, spears, spears and clubs available in Pacific. Because of the importance of Manu'a, especially in the Samoan area, it has been suggested as Havai'iki by some historians.[27]

Over time the Tu'i Manu'a declined in importance as ancient Polynesia declined and the colonial powers began to dominate the many islands. The last Tu'i Manu'a ceded the Manu'a Islands to American Samoa in 1904. He died on April 2, 1909 and stipulated in his will that he would be the last Tu'i Manu'a and that the title should die with him.

Although Manu'a is a remote backwater of American Samoa today, it is still revered by many Samoans, though it has lost its importance to the rest of Polynesia.

It is interesting to look at the legends of the Tu'i Manu'a and the importance of the ancient obsidian trade. Many valuable stones were traded from island to island by the ancient Polynesians, including jade from the South Island of New Zealand, basalt tools, and obsidian blades from Manu'a. Legend says that the small island group of Manu'a once ruled the entire central Pacific, including Hawai'i, Tahiti, Kiribati, Tonga, Samoa, New Zealand and presumably Rapa Nui and Fiji. The great double-canoes would arrive at the southern beach on Ofu to pay their respects to the Tu'i Manu'a and offer trading items to him in return for the valuable obsidian.

The Tu'i Manu'a also had his own great fleet of ships which anchored seasonally on the islands and went on long trading voyages in all directions. It is quite possible that the Tu'i Manu'a hired mercenaries and sailors from other islands for his merchant voyages.

The actual island home of the Tu'i Manu'a was the island of Ta'u. The highest mountain in Samoa, Mount Lata, (995 meters or 3,264 feet) was a sacred mountain, possibly because of the obsidian "mines." From Ta'u the Ta'i Manu'a practiced his magic powers such as invisibility and flying. The last Tu'i Manu'a was buried at Luma, the village where Margaret Mead wrote *Coming of Age in Samoa* in 1925.

Many Pacific islands have legends of flying men and "bird men." It is interesting to wonder whether the legends of ancient India and China about ancient flying vehicles or chariots can be associated with the legends of flight in the Pacific. The ancient Hindus called these ancient flying craft "vimanas" and their use is chronicled in many authentic Hindu texts and epics including *The Ramayana*.[37]

Did ancient vimanas visit visit the Tu'i Manu'a on Ta'u? Perhaps they then took the king to other islands such where other legends of flying men are told? An extraordinary concept!

The Aroi Sun Kingdom of Polynesia

Throughout Polynesia are *marae*, truncated, pyramidical platforms often built out of large stone blocks. What is their purpose?

W. H. R. Rivers has this to say on the subject in the *American Anthropologist*, (1915, volume 17, pages 431-445): *The conclusion so far reached is that the secret rituals of Oceania which have the sun as their object belong to an immigrant culture which has come from a widely distant part of the world. I have now to consider whether it is possible that this same people may have been the architects of the stone buildings and images which form so great a mystery of the is-*

Manaia, chief's son with war club.

lands of the Pacific.

Here again I will begin with eastern Polynesia. The Areoi societies held their celebrations in an enclosure called *marae* or *marai* at one end of which was situated a pyramidal structure with steps leading to a platform on which were placed the images of the gods during the religious celebrations of the people. The *marae* was used for religious ceremonial unconnected with the Areoi societies, but there seems to be no doubt that the Areois were of especial importance in connection with it. In the pyramid of the *marae* we have one of the best examples of the megalithic architecture of Polynesia. One such pyramid in the western part of the island of the island of Tahiti was 267 feet in length and 87 feet in breadth at the base. All were built of large stones without cement, but so carefully shaped that they fitted together closely and formed durable structures.

In the Marquesas, another home of the Areois, there were platforms similarly constructed a hundred yards in length, and many of them shaped and closely-fitted blocks of which these structures were composed were as much as eight feet in length. On these platforms were pyramidal 'altars' and they were surrounded by enormous upright stones. This association of the distribution of the Areois with the presence of megalithic structures suggests that the immigrants to whom I have ascribed the cult of the sun may also have been the people who introduced the art of building the stone structures which have so greatly excited the wonder of visitors to Polynesia.

The part of the Pacific Ocean where these stone structures have reached their acme in size and complexity is the Caroline Islands. If there be anything in my hypothesis, we should expect here also to find manifestations of the religious ideas of those who founded the Areoi societies, and they are not lacking. In the Mariana or Ladrone islands there were associations of persons which seem to furnish an intermediate condition between the Areois of Tahiti and the occupants of the clubhouse of Melanesia. We know very little about these associations, but their relation to the Areois of the east is shown clearly by the name they bore, Urritois or Ulitaos,

The last Tu'i Manu'a, Chris Young.

which is merely another form of the Tahitian word, Areoi, the latter word having suffered the elision of a consonant so frequent in Polynesia. Similar associations flourished in the Carolines, and though we know still less of them than of the Urritois of the Ladrones, we can be confident that they had a similar character. Societies very closely related to the Areois thus existed in this region in conjunction with stone structures similar to those of eastern Polynesia.

There is a remarkable point of similarity between the traditions concerning the origins of these stone structures and of the Areoi societies of Tahiti. The ruins of Nan-Matal (sic) on the east coast of Ponape in the Carolines are reputed to have been built by two brothers, Olochipa and Olochopa. In the tradition of the foundation of the Areois of Tahiti, a very prominent part was taken by two brothers, Orotetefa and Urutetefa. The interchanges between r and l, t and ch and p and f are so frequent in Oceania as to suggest that these two pairs of names are variants of one original, so that we should have in the traditions of these two groups of islands nearly four thousand miles apart a most striking similarity of the names of pairs of brothers to whom prominent features of the culture are ascribed. In one case the brothers founded societies whose aim it was to celebrate the annual changes of the sun, while rude stone buildings were the handiwork of the others.

A recent account by Hambruch shows that the resemblance between the Ponape and Tahiti names is not quite as close as would appear from previous records. Hambruch calls the two founders of the stone building, Sipe and Saupa but to put against this, he states that the place, Matolenim, where the structures were, was formerly called sau nalan which means "the sun."

Though the resemblance in the names of the two culture heroes of Ponape and Tahiti is not as close as once seemed to be the case, it cannot be neglected. It may be that the two words have some meaning which would reduce the importance of the similarity, but taken in conjunction with the close resemblance of the names of the societies in the two places, it affords striking corroborative evidence supporting the conclusion suggested by the distribution of societies and monuments that both are the work of one people.

"If the stone monuments and secret societies of Polynesia have had a common source, we should expect to find an association between the two elements of culture in Melanesia, and so it is. We know of stone structures in several parts of Melanesia, viz., the northern New Hebrides, Santa Maria in the Banks islands, Loh in the Torres islands, Ysabel in the Solomons, and Fiji. The Banks and Torres islands and the northern New Hebrides are strongholds of the secret cults, and though the only island in the Solomons in which we know of the existence of secret societies is Florida, there is a definite tradition that this society came to Florida from Ysabel. The distribution of stone structures in Melanesia is just as it should be if the ghost societies and the stone buildings were the work of one and the same people.

The evidence for the connection of stone structures with secret societies is even more definite in Fiji. The Nanga societies of Viti Levu take this name from their meeting places, oblong enclosures, consisting of two or more compartments, surrounded by stone walls. The resemblance of these enclosures to the marae of Polynesia has struck more than one observer and the similarity extends to detail. At one end of each main compartment of the nanga there were truncated pyramids which served as platforms, evidently representatives of the pyramids of the marae of Tahiti measured by Captain Cook. Further, both marae and nanga were oriented with their long axes east and west, though the two differ in that the pyramids were at the western end of the marae and at the eastern end of the nanga.

There is thus a remarkable correspondence between the distribution of stone structures and secret societies in Oceania which

Taupou, daughter of a High Chief.

points strongly, if not yet decisively, to the introducers of the secret cult of the sun having been the architects of the stone buildings which form one of the chief mysteries of the islands of the Pacific.

It is even possible that we may have here the clue to the greatest mystery of all, the great stone statues of Easter Island. There is reason to suppose that these statues are not so unique as is often supposed. According to Moerenhout, similar statues, though not so large, exist in the islands of Pitcairn and Laivaiva. He

believes that such colossal figures once existed in many other islands, but have been destroyed or have fallen into ruins. In the Marquesas and Society islands, also, stone figures in human form have been found which are sufficiently like those of the smaller and more eastward islands to suggest a common origin. Moerenhout believes that such stone figures and statues had a common meaning and were all representatives of beings called titi whose function it was to mark the limits of the sea and land, to maintain harmony between the two elements and prevent their encroachment upon one another. I venture, though very diffidently, to extend the comparison. At one end of a clubhouse of Santa Maria in the Banks islands there are ancient stone figures which, in one respect at least, resemble the colossal statues of Easter island. In each instance the head is covered. This head-covering is very frequent in one variety of the representations of the human figure found throughout Melanesia, and is almost certainly connected with the importance of head-coverings in the ritual of the secret societies. It is therefore of interest that a head-covering should be a prominent feature of the statues of Easter island. Such a point of resemblance standing alone would have little significance, but taken in conjunction with the other correspondences and similarities pointed out in this paper, we must not ignore the possibility that we may have here only another expression of the art of the people I suppose to have introduced the cult of the sun into Oceania.

I cannot consider here how far it is possible to connect the stone work and sun-cult of Oceania with the megalithic monuments and sun-cults of other parts of the world. Megalithic monuments elsewhere are associated with a cult of the sun and the occurrence of this association in the islands of the Pacific Ocean must serve to strengthen the position of those who hold that the art of building megalithic monuments has spread from one source. I must be content here to mention certain mega-

lithic monuments of Polynesia which raise a difficulty.

The island of the Pacific which holds examples of megalithic structures most closely resembling those of other parts of the world is Tongatapu, where there are trilithic monuments so like those of Europe that the idea of a common source must rise to the mind of even the most strenuous advocate of independent origin. It is not possible at present to bring these monuments into relation with those of other parts of Oceania by connecting them with a cult of the sun, but Hambruch tells us that tradition points to the builders of the stonework of Ponape having come from Tonga. It may be that Tongatapu forms the intermediate link between the stonework of the Carolines and the megalithic monuments of other parts of the world.

I have dealt elsewhere with the relation between these Tongan monuments and the pyramids of other parts of Oceania, and have suggested that these two ancient forms of monument may be expressions of the ideas of two different streams of the megalithic culture. I cannot deal with this matter here; to do so would take me far beyond the relation of sun-cult and megaliths which is the subject of this article.[83]

The notion of a sun-worshipping religion—or even a secret society—that existed throughout the Pacific is very intriguing. That an organized society of traders and navigators worshipped the sun and built great megalithic cities, pyramids, and platforms throughout the Pacific was an astounding thought! Who, then, would have been these "Vikings of the Sunrise," as Sir Peter S. Buck romantically called them? Dare I say that they had affinity with the sun-worshipping societies in India, the Middle East, Africa, Egypt and Peru? As tall, bearded, navigators of the world, they were probably a combination of Egyptian, Libyan, Phoenician, Ethiopian, Greek and Celtic sailors from the Mediterranean area in combination with Indo-Europeans from the Indian subcontinent. According to Polynesian legend, these sailors also had the famous "long ears" that are well known on both Rapa Nui and Rarotonga.

Raiatea, Savaii and Havai'iki

Maraes abound all throughout the Society Islands, there being at least thirteen marae-pyramids on Bora Bora, 28 on the island of Maeva, plus a number on both Huahine and Moorea. Unquestionably the most important island is that of Raiatea, the second largest of the group. By tradition it was the first island settled by the Polynesians, and it was from Raiatea that the great migrations traditionally set out from to the far corners of Polynesia, including Hawaii, Easter Island and New Zealand. For this reason, it is sometimes thought that the ancient and mysterious Havaiki was the island of Raiatea.

This is a controversial point, eloquently argued by Edward Dodd, in his book *Polynesia's Sacred Isle*.[42] Raiatea is the religious center of Polynesia and is unique for the sacred flower, the *tiare apetahi* which only grows on the slopes of the volcano Temehani. A white flower with five fragile petals, it cannot be transplanted and only grows at 2000 feet on the slopes of the volcano. Even efforts to transfer the flower by helicopter to a similar altitude on Tahiti have failed.

Also inexplicable is the fact that there are only two relatives of this strange and unique flower: the *apetahia longistigata* is also found at high altitudes of 3000 feet in the Marquesas, 500 miles to the northeast of Raiatea and *apetahia margaretae* occurring on the small island of Rapa (also called Rapa Iti) some 500 miles to the southeast, a remote spot at the very southern end of the Tubuai (also called Austral) Island group.

In his book about the rare flower and Raiatea, Edward Dodd searches for the solution to the puzzle of the distribution of the strange, sacred plant. His answer is that in the remote geological past (millions of years ago, he surmises) the Pacific consisted of "land bridges" and "an erstwhile huge island that the Tuamotu archipelago must very probably have been some 60 million years ago. Those 80 odd atolls, great and small, must at one time have been lofty mountain peaks, very possibly joined together at their bases by valleys and ridges. The whole mass would have run a thousand miles in length, northwest to southeast and 3 hundred miles in breadth. Can one imagine the island of Madagascar, there in the middle of the ocean those millions of years ago? It would have been lavishly populated with plants and birds insects and surrounded by myriads of fish.

"Then it starts of sink, the whole of it (or rather the tectonic plate on which its volcanoes have erected themselves). Over the aeons it subsides until only the tips of the highest mountain peaks show above the level of the sea.

"...So the ancestress of our *Apetahia* could conceivably have evolved on the huge lost island of 'Tuamotua,' dispersed her offspring as she sank below the waters to her younger neighbors, north, south and west before she slipped to her watery grave. They in turn would have adapted themselves differently to their different environments. Many cousins on in-between islands would have dropped out of the race...."[42]

And so Dodd finds the solution to the distribution of these three flowers to be, well, he won't quite say it, but his theory is a lost continent in the Pacific! He knew better than to mention a lost continent, this is the kiss of death in academic and scientific circles, as many authors have had the the misfortune to find out. Not being a geologist, he briefly discusses continental drift and the concept of Gondwanaland, but does not understand the subtle paradoxes in the changes of the earth. Indeed, Dodd's "lost island of Tuamotua" might well have gone down far more recently than millions of years ago.

Perhaps the lost land of Havai'iki, Havaiki, Havai'iki or Hawai'iki (all various spellings for the same place) was a now sunken land around the Tuamotus, a sunken area between the Western Samoan island of Savai'i and Upolu or even around the island of Manu'a. Or was it a legendary homeland to the far west, ancient India or even Egypt? Only the ancient gods of the Pacific, Maui and his companions, can tell us.

The Samoan board game known as *Lafoga*. Played by chiefs and nobility, shell money was thrown on a special mat. The ancient Egyptians, Hindus and Indonesians all played similar board games.

A sign welcomes the visitor to Mu'a.

One of the pyramids at Mu'a, now overgrown and part of a landowner's backyard.

Another of the pyramids at Mu's houses numerous and ruined temple-tombs stand beneath

The largest of the stone blocks at Mu'a. One can see how is has been split by and earthquake. On the far right is the unusual notching in the stone.

A close-up of the unusually notched stones.

One of the over grown pyramid's at Mu'a.

The unusually notched blocks seen from the backside of the massive wall.

One of the Langi platform at Lapaha.

A close-up of one of the walls at Lapaha with the perfectly fitted slabs. The stairs were made recently.

Close-up of some of the blocks at the Langi at Lapaha. This unusual stone in the middle has apparently been split by earthquakes

More of the terraced walls at Lapaha. The light colored slab on the top tier has a ribbed pattern worked into the stone. Note the fine stone workmanship.

The amazing Ha'amonga Trilithon known as The Burden of Maui

The massive lintel of the trilithon in fitted into notches on the upright stones.

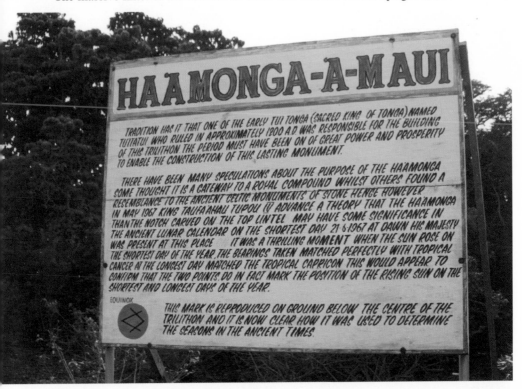

The government sign at the site declaring it an astronomical observatory. The marks on the top of the lintel are in the left corner of the sign.

The uncovered stone pyramid of Candi Sukuh in central Java, Indonesia.

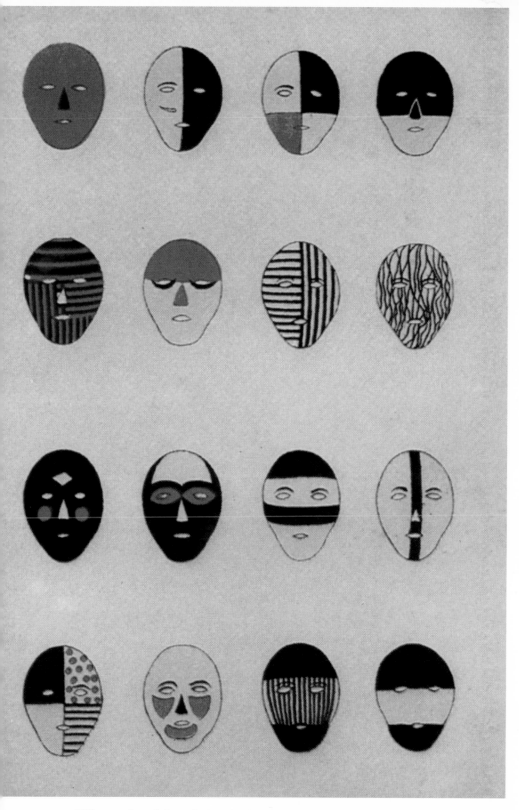

Fijian modes of the painting the face, probably also used in Tonga.

Two old men were common in Fiji.

The glass etching of the Polynesian "god" Wakea at the St. Faith Church in Rotorua, New Zealand. Here he is represented as walking across the waters of Lake Rotorua.

Thor Heyerdahl excavating one of the giant statues at Rapa Nui. These statues were buried up to their necks in soil, testifying that they are thousands of years old. Photo courtesy of thor Heyerdahl.

Rare photos of the massive granite walls found on the high slopes of Mount Koscuasko in Australia. These huge blocks may be natural or they may be artificial. If natural, they are a bizarre formation and if artificial, they may be remains of ancient megalithic construction such as in Peru and Bolivia. Photos courtesy of Ray Morcan

The Author, Rex Wailes, in a Gully surrounded by overwhelming lianas and Kaurie-trees or Wells in New Zealand

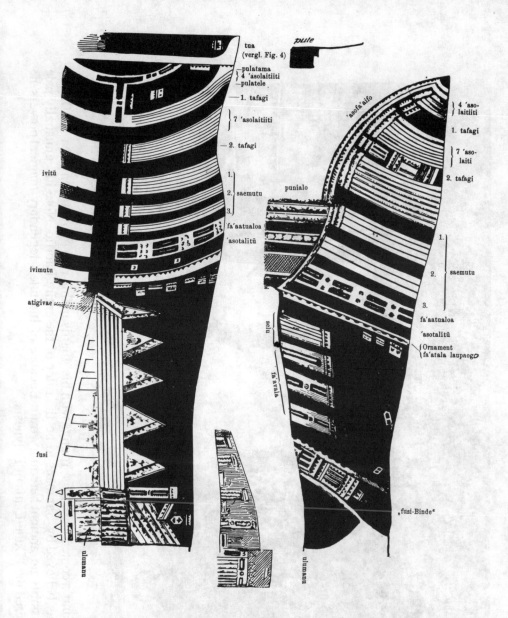

Samoan tattoo patterns on the upper thighs were highly intricate and were a form of insignia with each pattern having various meanings.

The last Tu'i Manu'a contender, Chris Young, with his guards in this rare photo taken circa 1910. The Tu'i Manu'a was believed by Samoans to be the ruler of the entire Pacific. Note his unusually pale complexion, possibly an ancient hereditary trait. Because of his title's legendary magical powers he might be considered the "Dalai Lama of Polynesia."

The Samoan chief Mata'afa Ali'i Sili and his court in this photo taken in the early 1900s.

Young Samoan chief, Samoa.

Samoa Islands.   Native Beauty.

Muir & Moodie   No. 6396.   Samoan Girl

Grüße von Samoa   *Kavabereitung*

"Telling Tales," Samoans.   *(Copyright.)*   *J. W. Waters, Suva, Fiji.*

Pago Pago Bay.

Greetings from Pago-Pago.

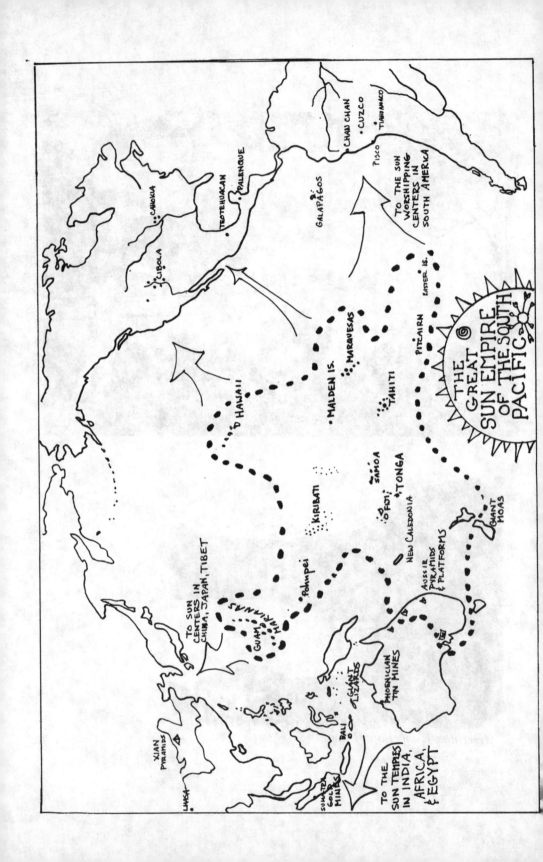

TATTOOED EASTER ISLANDER

TATTOOED MAORI, showing curvilinear
designs peculiar to New Zealand
Drawn by General G. Robley in 1865

Glass etching of Wakea walking on the waters of Lake Rotorua from the St. Faith Church of Rotorua, New Zealand.

Undeciphered Maori writing from the rare Chilean book, *La Isla de Pascua Y sus Misterios* by Dr. Stephen Chauvet.

A MARA.

Standing stones and warriors on Tongareva. From *Wild Life Among the Pacific Islanders* (1867).

THE RIVAL CHIEFS.

Two rival chiefs meet for battle on Tongareva. From *Wild Life Among the Pacific Islanders* (1867).

INVASION OF TAUTUA.

Tongarevan warriors prepare to be attacked. Note the defensive wall of an enclosure used by the warriors. From *Wild Life Among the Pacific Islanders* (1867).

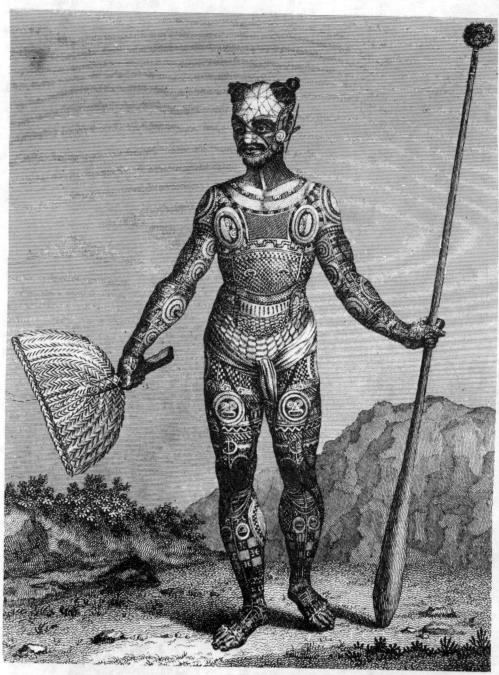

A man from the Marquesas with a full body tattoo. Portions of the man look like he is a living board-game, his forehead appears almost like a star-chart or map of sorts. A good example of the complexity of Marquesan tattooing.

An old print of a double-canoe of Rarotonga.

PAVED ROAD OF THE MARAE OF TANGAROA IN RAROTONGA

John Macmillan Brown's photo of the megalithic road that encircles Rarotonga. It is unique in Polynesia.

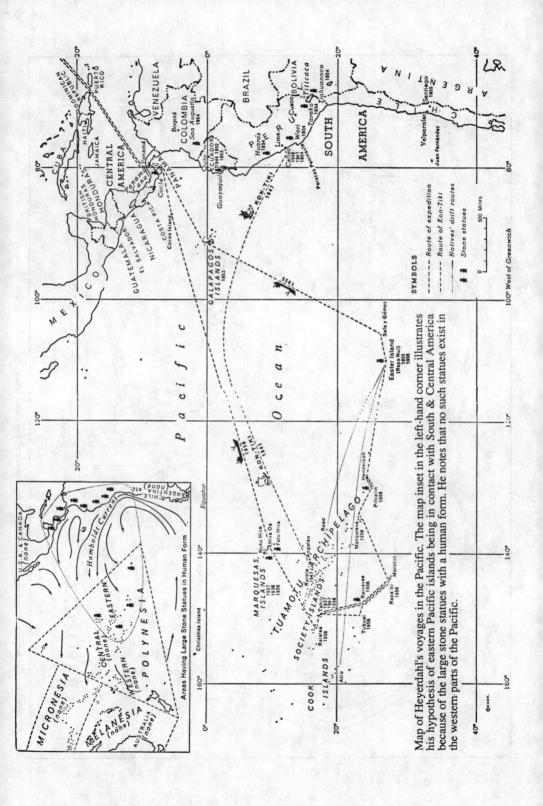

Map of Heyerdahl's voyages in the Pacific. The map inset in the left-hand corner illustrates his hypothesis of eastern Pacific islands being in contact with South & Central America because of the large stone statues with a human form. He notes that no such statues exist in the western parts of the Pacific.

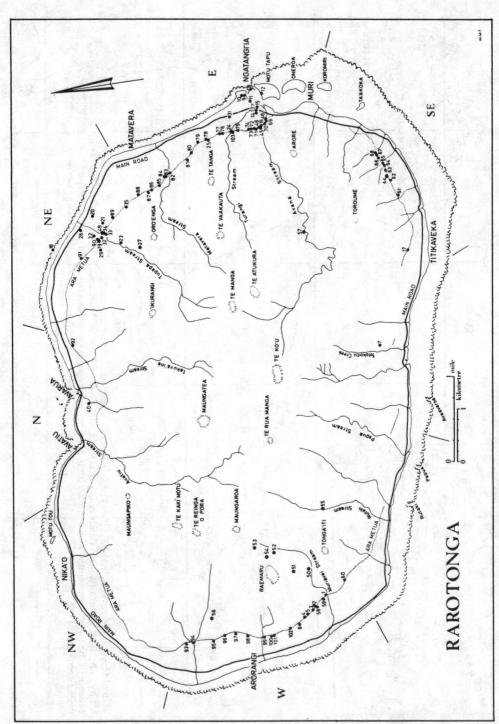

Site location map of Rarotonga, showing surviving course of the Ara Metua.

CHAPTER 5
RAROTONGA &
OTHER ISLANDS

Within the circle of the sea,
It holds a fish of note.
It holds a fish
O'er which the rainbow arches,
Spanning the immensity of Ocean.
It is—my land.
—Aitutaki Chant, *quoted by Peter Buck.*

Rarotonga is the largest of the Cook Islands, an independent nation with close ties to New Zealand. Rarotonga is a high volcanic island with fertile soil that rises up to 652 meters out of the ocean. Other mountainous Cook Islands include Aitutaki and Nassau, while other islands are typical low atolls such as Mangaia, Penrhyn, Atiu and Palmerston.

Rarotonga means "Far South" in most Polynesian dialects, and reflects some association with Tongatapu, or "Sacred South." One old name for Rarotonga is *Te Pukai Taringa o Papa*—The Ear Lobes of Papa. Piercing the ear and extending the earlobe was an old Maori custom in Rarotonga as well as Rapa Nui (Easter Island), ancient India and Peru. The statues of Rapa Nui have elongated ears and a legendary war was once fought on the island between the "long ears" and the "short ears." The dialect of Rarotonga is also said to be very close to the vernacular of Rapa Nui.

One Rarotongan tradition relates that Tangiia, a Tahitian navigator, and Karika, a warrior from Samoa, were the leaders of the two great migration which settled Rarotonga many hundreds, if not thousands of years ago.

Rarotonga has an important megalithic road which once circled the island, as well as other stone platforms, or marae, on other islands. Says Peter Bellwood in his book *The Polynesians*,[4] "The Cook Islands actually comprise two groups of islands. The northern Cooks are all atolls, basically eastern Polynesian in culture apart from Pukapuka, which on linguistic grounds would seem to have been settled from Samoa. These northern islands have few archaeological remains, although Penrhyn has many marae similar to those of the Tuamotus. The southern Cooks are rather more important, and these are nearly all volcanic islands, the largest being Rarotonga, Aitutaki and Mangaia. These islands have long been of importance for studies on ethnology and traditions in Polynesia, and Rarotonga in particular has a splendid tradition of woodcarving."

While the Cook Island group must have been originally settled during the Lapita pottery period, and was further linked to such isolated islands as the Rapa Iti in the Austral Group and Rapa Nui (Easter Island), the islands had fallen into isolation from the rest of Polynesian by the time of the European exploration, though other Polynesians were aware of the islands.

Bellwood claims, "At European contact they showed no real unity of culture, since they are separated from each other by quite large distances, and it is rather hard to generalize about them in the sense that one can generalize about the more homogeneous Society Islands. The southern Cooks supported a number of independent chiefdoms— generally several on an island—and traditional history is replete with accounts of local warfare. This was particularly the case on Mangaia, where political control was vested in the hands of a succession of warrior chiefs, who distributed lands among their followers until they in turn were deposed. Rarotonga had three main tribal areas and four titled paramount chiefs, and was politically more stable then Mangaia despite prolonged periods of fighting."[4]

Rarotonga and the other islands are thought to have been settled from Tahiti and eastern Polynesia, but are paradoxically closer to western Polynesian islands such as Samoa and Tonga. Says Bellwood, "Traditions and

A Rarotongan chief.

archaeology suggest that the southern Cooks were settled late in the first millennium A.D., perhaps from the Societies, with a possibility of a secondary settlement from Samoa to Rarotonga."[4]

Curiously, Bellwood does not even mention any contact with Tonga, the island the Rarotonga is virtually named after. Tonga is such an important island in ancient Polynesia, it is conspicuous when it is left out of the modern-day historian's explanations for the history of the Pacific. Tongan double-canoes were the last of the great canoes still being made in the Pacific at the time of European expansion. With the pyramid-temples, navigation school at Ha'amonga a Maui, and the huge fleet of ships that anchored in the lagoon, Tonga was continually sending ships out into the Pacific. Many of these ships naturally stopped in Rarotonga and from Rarotonga they would voyage south to New Zealand or east to Rapa Iti, Rapa Nui and Peru. Rarotongan tradition holds that Ngataniia bay on the western shore was the assembly point from which the Maoris began their voyages into New Zealand.

Ancient Structures and the Southern Route To Rapa Nui

Rarotonga was apparently an important southern island on the routes more important islands such as Rapa Iti and Rapa Nui, as well as New Zealand. Rarotonga would be an ideal stopping point for canoes from Tahiti going to New Zealand. Therefore, most have tagged the Cook Islands with a decidedly eastern Polynesian culture, simply because this was last migratory invasion to take place, circa 900 A.D.

Previously, huge fleets sailed regularly from such giant naval bases as Raiatea, Rapa Iti, Savai'i and, of course, the lagoon at Tongatapu. One important maritime route controlled by these ancient navigators was the route to Central and South America. This profitable trade route made Rapa Nui (Easter Island), one of the most remote islands in the world, an important supply base for long voyages in the eastern Pacific. The southern route to South America followed the natural currents which allowed a ship to leave Rapa Nui and be automatically taken to the western coast of South America. The ship followed the natural current north up the coast, which is largely desert, until one comes to the Candle-Stick-of-the Andes at Pisco, Peru. Here, a gigantic candlebra-sign is carved into a hillside which can be seen from far away at sea.

After trading with gold and metal rich Peruvians, the ship could continue north up the coast and then back out into the Pacific to follow the current back west to the Marquesas or northern Tuamotu Islands. From these islands the trip back to Raiatea, Samoa and Tonga was familiar and easy.

The Cook Islands have a number of stone platforms and other stone works, but it is on Rapa Iti and Rapa Nui that the large forts and gigantic statues and megalithic platforms are to be found. The large stone ceremonial platforms, maraes, are highly similar from Rarotonga to Tahiti and the Tuamotus. In the Marquesas, Tonga and Rapa Nui, they are much bigger, often on a colossal scale. Bellwood states in *The Polynesians*, "The marae architecture of the southern Cooks varies from island to island. On Rarotonga, structures with rectangular courts and ahu approximate to the general Tahitian fashion, although *ahu* are here often absent, and the courts themselves may be terraced into a series of steps on sloping ground. Uprights are also rather rare on Rarotonga, and there is a very marked difference here with the marae of Aitutaki, which were entirely without demarcated courts and ahu, and comprised one or more lines of large uprights. The marae of Paengariki on Aitutaki consisted of over sixty uprights about 2 meters in height arranged in six parallel rows; the total area covered being a rectangle of 80 by 40 meters. Although now in ruins, this structure

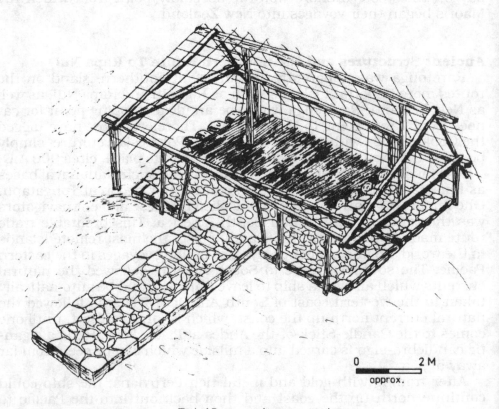

0   2 M
approx.

Typical Rarotongan house construction.

must one have been a very impressive sight. Finally, the Mangaian marae, and those of Atiu, consisted of simple earthen terraces faced with shaped slabs of reef coral, sometimes with rows of uprights on their tops. Some of the Mangaian monuments are closely paralleled in Rurutu,

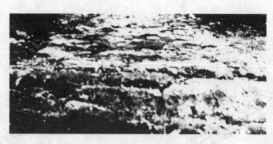
A portion of the Ara Metua.

and some prehistoric contact is possible."[4]

Rarotonga and Polynesia's Ancient Roads

Rarotonga's most famed ancient structure is the megalithic road which once encircled the entire island. It was paved with perfectly fitting slabs in some sections, but little of it can be seen today because it has been paved over by a modern road.

Rarotonga's ancient megalithic road is called the *Ara Metua*. The *Ara Metua* road on Rarotonga is essentially an island circuit road that goes around the island. It is inside of the new, paved road that rings the island today, and many parts of it are still used. In *The Polynesians*,[4] Bellwood wrote that "Most of the settlement was on this coastal plain, but concentrated along a road, called the Ara Metua, which ran right around the island linking the tribal districts, and which was paved in some sectors."

Curiously, one would expect this road to go along the coastline, where it was often assumed that the island population lived, but that is not the case. "The road ran around the inland edge of the coastal strip rather than along the coast itself, and this position was certainly chosen purposefully; the Rarotongan coast is subject to occasional hurricanes, and since the inhabitants utilized the mountain and valley regions quite commonly, they may have located their houses and their road in such a position that access time to all resources, including the sea, would be reduced to a rough minimum," says Bellwood.

Roger Duff in *Prehistory of the Southern Cook Islands*[85] confirms that sections of the road were of finely cut and fitted blocks of stone: "At every point where paving could be positively attested, it comprised flat slabs of basalt laid to form a continuous sheet of cobbling. In one or two places isolated slabs of coral were found embedded in the modern road surface. It is not clear whether this represents the remains of ancient paving or modern road repairs, but the latter is probably more likely. In several other localities there were extensive stretches of basalt or coral gravel. Generally such places gave little or no evidence of paving, and it may be that anciently extensive stretches of the Ara Metua were groveled rather than paved. Equally however the

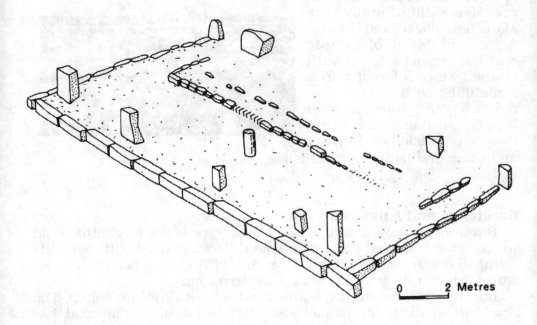

0 — 2 Metres

gravel may represent a relatively recent surface laid for wheel traffic."

Says Duff about the kerbing (or curbing) that ran along the side of road, "Particularly in the Tupapa area but quite frequently elsewhere between Avana and Black Rock, the kerbing was composed of neatly fitted blocks of prismatic basalt laid closely together, giving a level and relatively even top line to the kerbing on both sides of the road. In most other places but particularly on the outskirts of Avarua the kerbing was formed from small rounded boulders selected to be of approximately the same size. In a few places somewhat pointed boulders gave a sawtooth profile to the kerbing. As noted above, in the three places where the space between the kerbing on opposite sides of the road could be measured, it was in each case very close to 3.2 metres, and it seems likely that this spacing was normal."[85]

At various sections along the road were occasional "boxes" that were enclosures outlined by kerb stones and containing stone "seats." These These rectangular enclosures would contain from one or two or even twelve seats and were sometimes associated with marae ceremonial platforms that were set off from the road.

Duff says that the road was probably used a functional road that went around the island linking important ceremonial sites and villages. In ancient times passage along the road was free and unrestricted, but travellers were not permitted to leave the road without passing the inspection of sentries posted at or by the major seats. One of the seats, the Arai-mimiti-tangata was the place to which prisoners taken in war were brought for judgment.

The age of the road is currently estimated by New Zealand archaeologists to be over 1000 years. The University of Auckland estimates has said that it is over a millennium in age but no firm date has been established and it may have existed in its original form thousands of years ago. The road was in use up to the time of European discovery and continual building and maintenance was still in evidence.

Most of this ancient road, if not all of it, has now been paved over by a modern asphalt road. Photos of these ancient sections of road still exist and they indicate the work of a fine rock mason much in the same manner as the work found on Rapa Iti and Tonga.

One wonders if there are not other roads on other Polynesian islands that are yet to be discovered? Due to sea level changes and local earthquakes, some roads may be underwater. Local rumor has it that the Tongan Island of Eua has an ancient road somewhere in the center of it. This road begins and ends in a remote area of Eua, which is a fairly large island, and may have been part of a road that went to some as yet unknown temple, marae or pyramid in the forest.

Rarotonga has a number of pyramid-platforms, like Malden Island and many Pacific islands, but perhaps the most interesting thing on the island is the imposing "Black Rock" standing alone in a green coral lagoon near the main town of Avarua. This strange formation has been radiometric dated as two and a half million years old! Legend says that it marks the spot where the spirits of deceased Rarotongan Polynesians pass on their way back to the legendary home-

The massive stone fort on Rapa Iti, similar in some ways to Machu Picchu.

land of Hawaiki.[79]

Terraced forts, similar in many ways to the famous mountain fortress of Machu Picchu in Peru, exist on Rapa Iti and in the Maungaroa Valley of Rarotonga. According to Bellwood, "Normally, the Rarotongan valleys were not settled densely, except for the Maungaroa Valley, on the western side of the island, where the members of one tribe occasionally retired to escape the depredations of their warlike neighbors. This remote valley still contains many finely paved house platforms and marae, and provides, with the Opunohu Valley and Vitaria, one of the best-preserved community patterns in Polynesia. The Maungaroa dwellings are quite nucleated owing to the scarcity of good level land, much of which was doubtless needed for cultivation, and the larger ones sat on paved platforms across the ends of long paved approach paths." Bellwood concluded that the platforms had been occupied up to 1823 from a period beginning in at least 1300 A.D.[4]

Another fascinating island with an usual road system is remote and deserted Malden Island, a low, barren and uninhabited island in the remote Line Islands of Kiribati. Malden Island is a bizarre island because, although it is uninhabited, it has an amazing complex of pyramids, platforms, roads that disappear into the ocean, megaliths and other strange stacks of stones!

Ancient Writing, Ceremonies and Ancient Rites

More is known about the ceremonies and beliefs of the Cook Islanders than most other Polynesian islands because of the amazing life of Maretu, born in Ngatangiia village, Rarotonga, about 1802. His father, Tuaivi Morea, was *komono* or sub-chief under Tangiiau Mataiapo and an outstanding warrior. He was also a cannibal.

The tribal wars fought throughout the Cook Islands had degraded into cannibalistic rites. Cut off from the central island groups like Tahiti, Samoa and Tonga, Rarotonga collapsed into petty wars and savagery, circa 1300 A.D. In 1823, Maretu was converted from his cannibal ways by the Tahitian missionary Papeiha and later by the London Missionary Society.

Maretu wrote a manuscript of his early life in the Rarotongan language. Maretu died in 1880 and it wasn't until a century later that his book was translated and published in English by Marjorie Tuainekore Crocombe. Crocombe's book, *Cannibals and Converts* was published by the University of the South Pacific in Fiji in a paperback edition in 1983.

Maretu's book gives us a fascinating look at a complex society where weddings were thrown with great pomp and a ceremony. Maretu helped various reverends and researchers draw up curious illustrations of the complex supernatural worlds that were nested around the earth. These supernatural dimensions included nine (or ten) planes of existence plus the belief in Awaiki, Hawaii, or Savai'i (Hawai'iki). Dead souls journeyed to the west. This drawing was first published in 1876.

Edward Dodd in *Polynesia's Sacred Isle*[42] publishes a similar old drawing from the Tuamotus showing the Polynesian creation of the world. It is particularly interesting because it shows the world created in nine layers or "planes" of existence. Published in the *Journal of the Polynesian Society* (1869) it is curious for two reasons: the drawing is in shape of a pyramid and this is also the typical Hindu creation belief, of nine (or seven, or sometimes thirteen) planes of existence. Similarly, many Bible scholars feel that the statement in *Genesis* of God creating the world in seven days is referring to seven planes of existence. Egyptians also believed this, and such doctrine is generally thought to have arrived from even more ancient civilizations. Egyptians and other early civilizations also believed that dead souls journeyed to the west with setting sun. Once again, we have a curious connection with both ancient Indian and Egyptian—a link with other Sun Kingdoms around the world, including Japan and Peru.

Writing, curiously enough, apparently existed in some parts of the

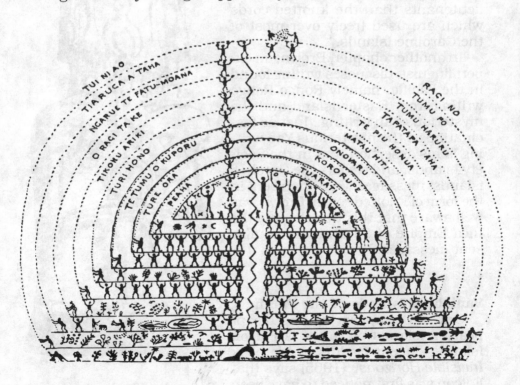

Polynesian concept of different planes of existence as recorded in the Tuamotus in 1869.

Pacific such as Rapa Nui, Fiji and Micronesia. We know that nearby civilizations to Polynesia had writing: Bali and Indonesia, ancient Cambodia and China, as well as Japan. The Mayans, Toltecs and Aztecs all had writing systems. The Peruvians also had writing but disallowed it, and afterwards used only a secret code and the knotted cords called quipus to keep messages on. The Polynesians and Chinese were also known to use memory systems of knotted cords.

Brown's *The Riddle of the Pacific*[1] goes on to mention in a chapter on subsidence in Micronesia the curious story of the little coral island of Oleai Atoll (now on maps as Woleai Atoll) to the east of Yap. "There I found," says Brown, "in 1913, script of some sixty characters, a syllabary quite unlike any other in the world. It was use by the young chief of the island and was known to only five on it (that is, it was known to only five persons on an island of about 600), though it was also in use in Faraulep, an islet about a hundred miles to the north-east. If this has any significance, it is that an archipelagic empire of considerable extent needed means of communication that would enable the central authority to keep in touch with its subordinates. Some maker or unifier of the island-empire needed a more explicit method of conveying his commands to his lieutenants than the knotted cords which are used freely over most of the Caroline Islands."

In another chapter, Brown, an expert linguist, discusses writing found in the Pacific, namely Rongo Rongo writing from Easter Island and the mysterious Yap writing. Just as fascinating as the mysterious Yap writing is his assertion that in the Society Islands, and well as the Caroline islands, messages were often sent in the form of knotted ropes. Brown was well aware that this was the way the Inca Empire of South America also sent messages.

Vanishing Islands of the Pacific

One of the appearing and disappearing islands of Tonga is Falcon Island. Vincent Gaddis in his book *Invisible Horizons*[11] (1965) says that Falcon was first noticed to have been

The backside of a Rapa Nui statue showing markings and belt that are similar to an Egyptian ankh.

raised as an island in 1885 when the coral shoal was measured at an incredible 290 feet above the ocean surface. During the following 13 years its two-mile-diameter mass disappeared. Says Gaddis, "It was reborn in 1927, and today is about 100 feet in height. Metis Island, 75 miles from Falcon, popped up in 1875, vanished in 1899."

Another disappearing island of Tonga is Onaneuse or Hunter Island, an island first reported in 1823 by Captain Hunter of the Donna Carmelita. The island was inhabited and was said to be at the lat.15° 31' S.; long. 176° 11' W. The nearest island is (was) Niaufou, the famous "Tin Can Island" of stamp collecting fame.

Says Karl Baarslag in *Islands of Adventure*,[12] "Captain Hunter said Onaneuse was inhabited by intelligent and cultivated Polynesians who had the curious custom of amputating the little finger of the left hand at the second joint. He added that the land was fertile, with plenty of coconut palms and breadfruit."[11, 12] Tongans also had this curious custom of amputating the little finger of the left hand at the second joint which was said to be a substitution of human sacrifice for a dying chief. Instead of a family being sacrificed on a funeral pyre when a chief died, the little finger of the left hand was cut off instead.

In *The Riddle of the Pacific*. Brown summed up his evidence for vanished islands. In Chapter VII entitled: *Subsidence Dominant In Polynesia & Micronesia*, Brown argues for the slow subsidence over thousands, even millions of years in the Pacific, and gives plenty of evidence for such subsidence. The formation of coral atolls, a geological mystery in themselves, requires both elevation and subsidence in their creation. Even phosphate islands like Nauru need to be submerged for a time and then uplifted, the nitrates leached out to form the rich phosphate deposits, he says.

Characters Used in Oleai Written by the Chief Egilimar.

na	tschra	rä		P N Runge	
goo	mmä	lüh			
dâa	tschä	sthah		EYE BROWN	
bä	moâ	töo			
tschroa	ro	wä		HONEI EGILIMAR	
nôo	ma	schä			
pui	boa	kä			
rü	tä	soâ		The mark ^ indicates accent	
ma	pä	bag			
bö	vôa	ku			
mä	schrü	schrö			
ngä	pu	gkaa			
boa	lö	rü			
warr	tüt	nga			
rêa	va	môo			
uh	lä	gä			
dôo	moi	du			

Brown relates one sad case in his book, that of the Tuanaki Islands southeast of Rarotonga, about half way to Mangaia. The island group consisted of three low-lying islands inhabited by Polynesians. They were unspoiled, but a sailor's account of life on the islands was given in the *Rarotongan Records* of the Rev. W. Wyatt Gill, published by the *Polynesian Society* of Honolulu in 1916. The sailor had lived on the island of Rurutu for six days, and himself was a Polynesian. In 1844 a missionary ship that was bound for the islands failed to locate them. It is believed they vanished in an earthquake between 1842 and 1884. Several former inhabitants of the Tuanaki Islands, who had left in their youth, died in Rarotonga during the present century.

It is said that the tall peak on the southern side of Rarotonga, "The Needle," was an important navigational beacon for the islanders who lived on the now sunken land of Tuanaki. This conspicuous peak is called Te Rua Manga which has the meaning of "the lair of the snake mackerel fish." This peak is also said to have been carved into the likeness of a faces which can be seen on the rock. Though they may be only natural formations that have an uncanny appearance of a human profile, it is believed by the islanders that they were artificially carved as signals to ancient mariners. In some ways the faces resemble the giant statues of Rapa Nui (Easter Island). No archaeological work as to whether there are rock chips at the base of the mountain has yet been done, and therefore whether the rock faces are natural or artificial has not been established.

Islands have even gone down in recent times, claims Brown. Vincent Gaddis relates some of the fascinating tales of "lost islands" in his book, *Invisible Horizons*.[11] The English pirate Captain Edward

A Manihikian bride wearing a traditional poncho. Ponchos were worn in Rarotonga as well as in South America and Mexico.

Davis discovered an island with "a long sandy beach and coconut palms" in 1687. A huge landmass stretching beyond the horizon lay beyond the sandy island. He gave the location as latitude 27° S and about five hundred miles west of the South American coast. Davis had ample provisions and was in a hurry, so he did not stop, however, the island was added to the charts. It was never seen again. In fact, Easter Island was discovered by the Dutch Navigator Roggeveen while searching for Davis Land, a vanished island.

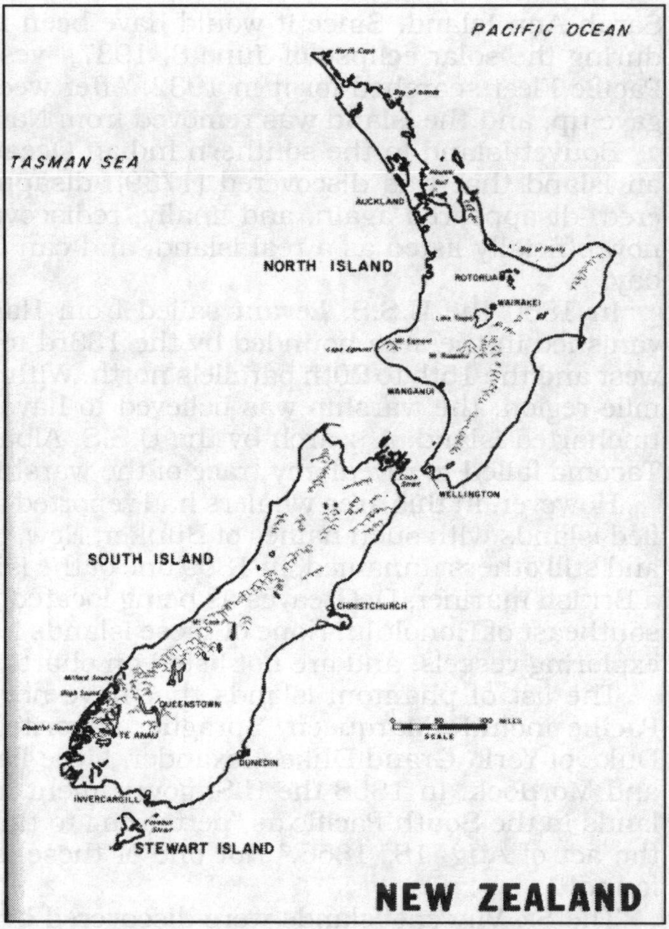

In 1802, a Captain Gwyn reported that the rocks of Sala-y-Gomez had been erroneously charted. He had found that the rocks were three hundred miles west and fifty miles south of Easter Island. Mariners made a search. The rocks were found at their charted location, while there was no trace of rocks at the location given by Gwyn. A similar island was reported in 1879 in the vicinity by an Italian Captain Pinocchio who named it after his vessel, the Podesta. Podesta Island, although appearing on charts, was never seen again and finally removed from Naval charts in 1935.[11]

Also near Easter Island, the English vessel S.S. Glewalon sighted an island in 1912. After all officers checked their calculations, they turned them over to harbor authorities. However the Chilean training ship Baquedano searched for the new island for three weeks without success. Soundings in the region revealed a depth of around ten thousand feet![109]

Another island northwest of Easter Island was listed on charts as

TASMAN SEA

NORTH ISLAND

SOUTH ISLAND

STEWART ISLAND

NEW ZEALAND

Sarah Ann Island. Since it would have been in the path of totality during the solar eclipse of June 8, 1937, vessels of the U.S. Navy Pacific Fleet searched for it in 1932. After weeks of searching, they gave up, and the island was removed from Naval charts.

Bouvet Island in the southern Indian Ocean is a famous case of an island that was discovered (1739), disappeared, was rediscovered, disappeared again, and finally, rediscovered once again. It is now officially listed as a real island, and can be found on maps today.

In 1860 the U.S.S. Levant sailed from Hawaii for Panama and vanished in the area bounded by the 133rd to the 138th meridians west and the 15th to 20th parallels north. Within this 30,000 square-mile region, the warship was believed to have been wrecked on an uncharted island. A search by the U.S.S. Albatross and the cruiser Tacoma failed to reveal any trace of the warship or of the islands.

However, in this area whalers had reported a number of unidentified islands with such names of Bunker, New, Sultan, Eclipse, Roca, and still others unnamed. In 1859 one of the islands was reported by a British mariner, DeGreaves as being located twelve hundred miles southeast of Honolulu. None of these islands has ever been found by exploring vessels, and are not listed on charts to this day.[11]

The list of phantom islands that have never been found in the Pacific include Marqueen, Sprague, Favorite, Monks, Dangerous, Duke of York, Grand Duke Alexander, Little Paternosters, Massacre and Mortlock. In 1858 the U.S. government listed over a dozen islands in the South Pacific as "pertaining to the United States under the act of Aug. 18, 1856." Not one of these islands has ever been found![11]

The St. Vincent Islands were discovered by Antonio Martinus in 1789 at lat 7° 21'N and long. 127° 4' W, and in 1824 a Father Santa Clara at the Rosario Mission near St. Francis Bay, California told a Captain Charles Morrell about the islands and that he had lived there for some time. They were inhabited, well-wooded and with good harbors. In 1825 Captain Morrell searched for the islands but all he could find was

A stone storehouse from Rotorua, New Zealand, now partially covered by a lava flow.

discolored water 120 fathoms deep. There were no other islands within hundreds of miles and Morell searched the area for over a month. The islands had vanished!

Gaddis goes on to list a number of "appearing and disappearing" islands between Alaska and Japan, many of them sighted during the war, and one larger than Guam, which have never been seen since. Most were reported from the air. A number of mysterious islands have been reported around Hawaii.

Perhaps the strangest story is the tale told by author Robert Casey in his classic 1931 book *Easter Island*[3] of a 20,000 ton round-the-world cruise ship from Britain that was to stop at Easter Island. On noon of a summer day in 1928 the captain and two British Naval Reserve officers were determining their position. They checked and rechecked their calculations. To their fantastic surprise, they concluded that Easter Island had vanished, as they were at the islands known location!

They went to the radio room and reported the astonishing news to the world and steamed on. In Valparaiso, Chile, the reported disappearance on an island that was their territory was greeted with genuine concern. A gunboat was sent out to the island to investigate the report, and ten days later arrived at the island, finding it in its same old place. The longitude and latitude had not changed one whit. Did Easter Island want to vanish?

The lost world of Polynesia continues to beckon from the past. The monumental remains that define Tonga, Samoa, Fiji and Rarotonga stand as testimony to the great empire that once existed throughout the Pacific. The many islands of Polynesia were once united in a central government, one that was once centered on Tonga.

Later, as this great maritime empire began to fragment, the various far-flung island groups were left in more or less isolation. Remote island groups like Hawaii and the Marquesas were largely cut off from the rest of Polynesia and regional capitals in Raiatea, Samoa and Rarotonga superseded Tongatapu. Tongatapu continued to influence nearby island areas such as Fiji, Rarotonga and Samoa and even at the time of the European exploration in the Pacific the giant Tongan double canoes were voyaging between these islands,

An ancient lintel found in the Awanui swamp, north of Auckland, now in the Auckland Museum. This unusual carving is unlike typical Maori style.

though the power of the Tu'i Tonga had been diminished.

The desperate isolation that some islands fell into reached its pinnacle at Rapa Nui. Rapa Nui had apparently been an important island stopping point on the trade route to and from South America, but one year the ships simply stopped coming. A breakdown in the central governments in Tonga, Samoa and Tahiti had caused the thriving sea trade to collapse. In desperation the Rapa Nui islanders carved gigantic statues as signs to passing ships which never came. Eventually a civil war on the island caused the virtual collapse of the stone cutting culture on that remote island.

Perhaps on soft moonlit nights in Tonga, Rapa Nui, Samoa or Rarotonga, when the light is just right, one can see the large fleet of double canoes sheltered in a lagoon waiting for the winds that would take them to the next island group. The legend of Tonga and great Polynesian empire of the Pacific lives on in the massive walls of the pyramids, platforms and other ancient structures of the islands.

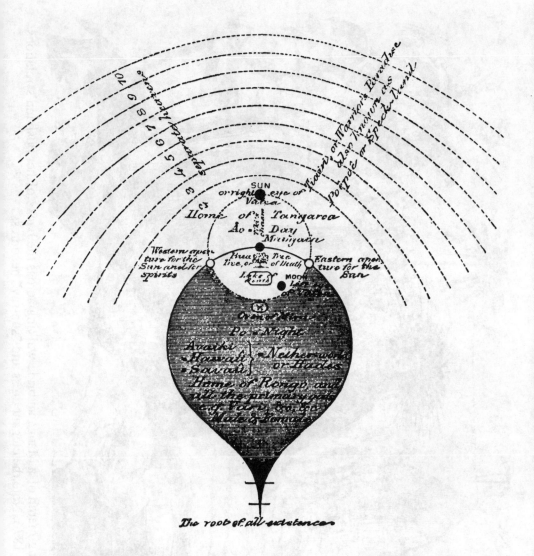

The traditional Mangaian conception of the supernatural world as published in 1876 by the Missionary Gill. There are ten planes of existence and world of the spirits is called Avaiki, Havaiki or Savaii. Havaiki is also the home of "Rongo".

A traditional wedding march of a Mangaian bride walking across the backs of her husband's relations as drawn by Gill in 1876. Note the elegant dress and "sun-ray" headdress.

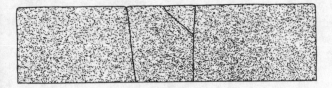

WESTERN WALL

NORTHERN WALL

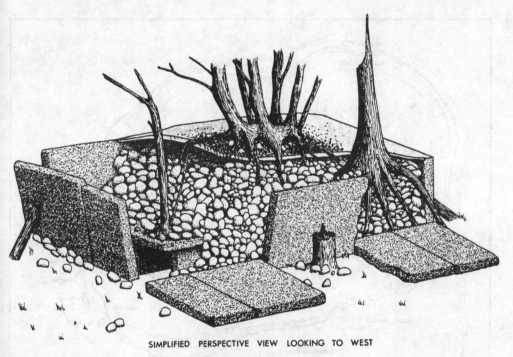

SIMPLIFIED PERSPECTIVE VIEW LOOKING TO WEST

Note the excellent stonework on these Rarotongan structures.
Small by Tongan standards, but highly similar.

PAIKEA
TOMB

VAULT

M.M.T.

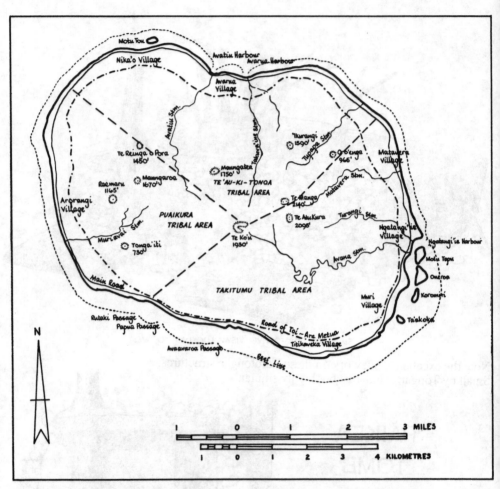

A map of Rarotonga showing the tribal areas and the Ara Metua.

View of a section of the Ara Metua, Rarotonga's unusual paved road.

A typical feature on the Ara Metua, a kerbing "box" containing a stone seat, this structure is associated with the title of Kainuku Ariki.

A photo of one of the meeting areas adjacent to the Ara Metua, this one known as Te Maru o Ta'iti. The title holder stands with a kava bowl and a stone pounder near the midpoint of courtyard. Stone seats can be seen on either side of him.

Soul Traps in Pukapuka

On Mangaia these "soul traps" or "spirit catchers" were hung from trees.

A walled enclosure used for a human sacrifice at Akaero on the island of Mangaia by Gill, 1876.

Two natives of Mangaia drawn by Gill in 1856. The man on the left with the long ear lobes and top knot hairstyle common on Rapa Nui. The man on the right wears the dress of a missionary pastor.

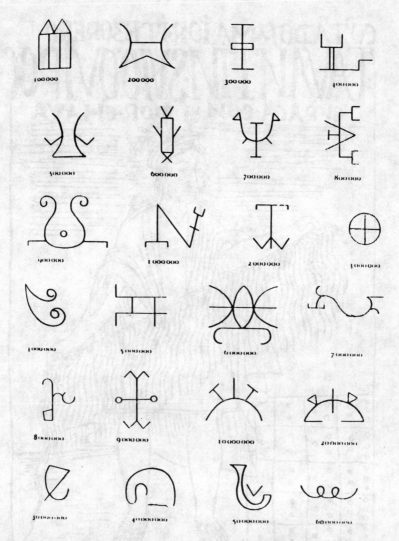

In 1908 the members of the Thilenius South Seas Expedition to the Micronesian atoll of Faraulep collected these symbols as part of the counting system used on the island. With numbers from 100,000 to 60 million, these numbers are so extremely high that they would no apparent use in the daily life of a small atoll and are apparently a legacy from a previous culture that once spanned the Pacific.

Inca quipu-camoyoc, quipu, and counting device. From
Poma de Ayala, Inca-Spanish chronicler, c. 1565.

The Realm of the Incas

COLOMBIA

ECUADOR

BRAZIL

PERU

PACIFIC OCEAN

Bahia

Valdivia

Pajaten

Trujillo

Chan Chan

Mochica u

Chavin

LIMA
Pachacamac

Machu Picchu
Sacsahuaman

Ollantaytambo
Pisac

Pisco

Paracas

Ica-Nazca

Cuzco

Tiahuanaco

Puno
Tiahuanaco

LA PAZ

The Inca Empire

QUITO
Manta
Valdivia

COLOMBIA

BRAZIL

Trujillo

PERU

Cuzco

BOLIVIA
LA PAZ

CHILE

Tucumán

SANTIAGO   ARGENTINA

Archaeological sites
Royal road of the Incas

0   100   200   300   400 Miles

0   200   400   600 Km.

Map of the priniciple Inca ports of Chan Chan, Pachacamac and Pisco.

Photos of items found at Thor Heyerdahl's dig in the Maldive Islands.
Note the pictographic scrip being used in the top right photo.

A long-ear of Easter Island with beard and feather crown, drawn on the spot during Captain Cook's visit.

From *Riddle of the Pacific* by John Macmillan Brown(1925)

Part of the mystery of Easter Island is that of "Royal Race" with long ears. Incas were often depicted as being a "Royal Race" with long ears. Buddha is usually depicted as having long ears, and it is a common motif in India.

The author at the massive, perfectly fitted stone platform of Vinapu. This platform and method of construction are unique to the island, but not unique in the world.

5 to 10 ton blocks of basalt are perfectly cut, dressed, and fitted at Vinapu. Note the rounded corner and lichen growth. Identical construction to this is found high in the Andes Mountains at Cuzco and Machu Picchu. Were they built by the same culture?

BIBLIOGRAPHY & FOOTNOTES

1. **The Riddle of the Pacific**, John Macmillan Brown, 1924, London. Reprinted by Adventures Unlimited Press, 1996.

2. **The Prehistoric Exploration and Colonisation of the Pacific**, Geoffrey Irwin, 1992, Cambridge University Press.

3. **Island Kingdom: Tonga Ancient & Modern**, I.C. Campbell, 1992, University of Canterbury, Christchurch, New Zealand.

4. **The Polynesians**, Peter Bellwood, 1978, Thames & Hudson, London.

5. **Island Kingdom: Tonga Ancient & Modern**, Ian C. Campbell, 1992, Canterbury University Press, Christchurch, New Zealand.

6. **Narrative of the United States Exploring Expedition**, Charles Wilkes, U.S.N., 1845, Lea & Blanchard Publishers, Philadelphia.

7. **Megaliths and Masterminds**, Peter Lancaster Brown, 1979, Charles Scribner's Sons, New York.

8. **The God-Kings & the Titans**, James Bailey, 1973, St. Martin's Press, New York.

9. **Man Across the Sea: Problems of Pre-Columbian Contacts**, edited by Riley, Kelley, Pennington & Rands, 1971, University of Texas Press, Austin and London.

10. **The Island Civilizations of Polynesia**, Robert Suggs, 1960, Mentor Books, New York.

11. **Invisible Horizons**, Vincent Gaddis, 1965, Ace Books, New York.

12. **Islands of Adventure**, Karl Baarslag, 1940, Farrar & Rhinehart, NY.

13. **Easter Island**, Robert Casey, 1931, Bobbs-Merrill Co., Indianapolis.

14. **Cannibals and Converts: Radical Change in the Cook Islands**, Maretu, 1983, University of the South Pacific, Suva, Fiji.

15. **Vikings Of the Pacific**, Peter H. Buck, 1938, University of Chicago Press.

16. **Lost Cities of China, Central Asia & India**, David Hatcher Childress, 1991, Adventures Unlimited Press, Stelle, Illinois.

17. **Fiji's Times**, Kim Gravelle, 1988, Fiji Times Press, Suva, Fiji.

18. **The Atlas of Archaeology**, 1982, St Martin's Press, NY.

19. **Ice, The Ultimate Disaster**, Richard Noone, 1982, Crown Publishers, New York.

20. **Hindu America?,** Chaman Lal, 1960, Bhavan's Book University, Bombay.

21. **Atlantis & the Giants,** Denis Saurat, 1957, Faber & Faber, London.

22. **Lost Cities of Ancient Lemuria & the Pacific,** D.H. Childress, 1988, Adventures Unlimited Press, Stelle, IL.

23. **Lost Cities of North & Central America**, D.H. Childress, 1992, Adventures Unlimited Press, Stelle, IL.

24. **The World of the Polynesians**, Antony Alpers, 1970, Oxford University Press, Auckland, NZ.

25. **Ancient Man: A Handbook of Puzzling Artifacts**, William Corliss, 1978, The Sourcebook Project, Glen Arm, MD.

26. **It's Still A Mystery**, Gebhart & Wagner, 1970, SBS, NYC

27. **Samoa: A Travel Survival Kit**, Deanna Swaney, 1990, Lonely Planet, Yarraville, Australia.

28. **History of Samoa**, Brother Fred Henry, 1930, 1 (reissued 1979), Commercial Printers, Apia.

29. **Lagaga: A Short History of Western Samoa**, Malama Meleisea, 1987, University of the South Pacific, Suva, Fiji.

30. **Mysteries of the Unexplained**, 1982, Reader's Digest, Pleasantville, NY.

31. **Millennia of Discoveries**, Alexander Y. Adams, 1994, Vantage Press, New York.

32. **Down Among the Wild Men**, John Greenway, 1973, Hutchinson, London.

33. **Arts & Crafts of Torres Strait**, David R. Moore, 1989, Shire Publications, Aylesbury, England.

34. **Tongan Astronomy**, T.H. Fale, 1990, Polynesian Eyes Foundation, Tonga.

35.**Through Polynesian Eyes**, T.H. Fale, 1989, Polynesian Eyes Foundation, Tonga.

36. **Science News**, Vol. 130, No. 21, Nov. 1986, page 333.

212

37. **Ramayana**, various translations, (U. of Calif. Press version by W. Buck, 1976)

38. **Legends of the World**, R. Cavendish, 1982, Orbis Publishing, London

39. **Lost City of Stone**, Bill S. Ballinger, 1978, Simon & Schuster, New York

40. **Lost Cities & Ancient Mysteries of South America**, D. H. Childress, 1986, AUP, Stelle, IL.

41. **Pale Ink**, Henriette Mertz, 1953, Swallow Press, Chicago.

42. **Polynesia's Sacred Isle**, Edward Dodd, 1976, Dodd, Mead & Co. New York.

43. **The Atlas of Archaeology**, 1982, St. Martin's Press, NYC

44. **The Maldive Mystery**, Thor Heryerdahl,1986, Adler-Adler, Bethesda MD

45. **Lost Worlds**, Alastair Service, 1981, Arco Publishing Co. NYC

46. **A Fragile Paradise**, Andrew Mitchell, 1989, Fontana/Collins, London.

47. **Pathways To the Tongan Past**, Dirk Spennemann, 1988, Tongan National Centre, Nuku'alofa.

48. **Pathways to the Tongan Present**, Kurt Düring, 1990, Scientific Society for the Pacific Islands, Nuku'alofa.

49. **Sea Routes to Polynesia**, Thor Heyerdahl, 1968, Allen & Unwin, London.

50. **Early Man and the Ocean**, Thor Heyerdahl, 1978, Doubleday, New York.

51. **American Indians in the Pacific**, Thor Heyerdahl, 1952, Allen & Unwin, London

52. **Shipping & Maritime Trade of the Indus People**, S.R. Rao, 1965, Expedition Journal, Philadelphia: University of Pennsylvania, Vol. 7, No. 3

53. **Lost Tribes & Sunken Continents**, Robert Wauchope, 1962, University of Chicago Press, Chicago.

54. **Aku-Aku**, Thor Heyerdahl, 1958, Rand McNally Co., Chicago, IL.

55. **Fatu Hiva**, Thor Heyerdahl, 1974, Doubleday and Co, NYC..

56. **Pyramids of Tucume**, Thor Heyerdahl, 1995, Thames & Hudson, London.

57. **Kon Tiki**, Thor Heyerdahl, 1950, Rand McNally Co., Chicago, IL.

58. **Kon-Tiki Man**, Christopher Ralling, 1990, BBC Books, London.

59. **The Lost Caravel**, Robert Langdon, 1975, Pacific Publications, Sydney.

60. **Strange World**, Frank Edwards, 1964, Bantam Books, New York.

61. **Stranger Than Science**, Frank Edwards, 1959, Bantam Books, NY.

62. **Wild Life Among the Pacific Islanders**, E.H. Lamont, 1867, Hurst & Blackett, London (reprinted 1994, University of the South Pacific, Suva).

63. **Technology In the Ancient World**, Henry Hodges, 1970, Marboro Books, London.

64. **Lost Cities & Ancient Mysteries of South America**, David Hatcher Childress, 1987, Adventures Unlimited Press, Stelle, Illinois.

65. **Lost Cities & Ancient Mysteries of Africa & Arabia**, David Hatcher Childress, 1990, Adventures Unlimited Press, Stelle, Illinois.

66. **Maori Origins and Migrations**, M. P. Sorrenson, 1979, Aukland University Press, Auckland.

67. **The Languages of the Pacific**, J.M. Brown, 1920, Auckland.

68. **Maori and Polynesian**, J.M. Brown, 1907, Auckland.

69. **Typee**, Herman Melville,1846, Signet Books, NYC.

70. **The Aryan Maori**, E. Treagar, 1885, Auckland.

71. **The Hidden Worlds of Polynesia**, Robert Suggs, 1962, Harcourt Brace,NYC..

72. **The Friendly Islanders**, Kenneth Bain, 1967, Hodder & Stoughton, London.

73. **Strange Facts & True About New Zealand**, Patricia Chapman, 1984, Dunmore Press, Palmerston North, NZ.

74. **He Walked the Americas**, L. Taylor Hansen, 1963, Amherst Press, Amherst, WI.

75. **No Moa**, Beverley McCulloch, 1982, Canterbury Museum, Christchurch

76. **America B.C.**, Barry Fell, 1976, Simon & Schuster, NYC.

77. **Argonauts of the Western Pacific**, Bronislaw Malinowski, 1922, E.P. Dutton & Co., New York.

78. **More Things**, Ivan T. Sanderson, 1969, Pyramid Books, NYC.

79. **South Pacific Handbook**, David Stanley, 1984, Moon Pub, Chico, CA.

80. **Assignment New Guinea**, Keith Willey, 1965, Jacaranda Press, Brisbane.

81. **INFO Journal**, No. 2, Autumn 1967, pp.15-16.

82. **Radiocarbon**, June 1966, Vol. 8, Yale University Press, New Haven, CT.Report on C-14 datings by the Centre des Faibles Radioactivities, C.N.R.S., Gif-sur-Yvette, Essonnes, France.

83. **Strange Artifacts**, William Corliss, 1974, The Sourcebook Project, Glen Arm, MD.

84. **Revue de a Societe d'Etudes Melanesiennes**, M. Chavalier, 1964, Noumea.

85. **Prehistory of the Southern Cook Islands**, Roger Duff, 1974, Canterbury Museum Bulletin #6, Christchurch.

85. **Feathered Gods and Fishhooks**, Patrick Vinton Kirch, 1985, U. of Hawaii Press, Honolulu.

From *Riddle of the Pacific* by John Macmillan Brown (1925)

A *langi*, OR TOMB OF THE TUITONGAS NEAR MUA, THE ANCIENT CAPITAL OF TONGATABU, WHEN PARTIALLY CLEARED OF ITS FOREST GROWTH

2598 "ZION" — NUKUALOFA — TONGA
BEATON BROS. DUNEDIN
COPYRIGHT

FOTOFILI
GOV. OF NIUAFOOU

REV. J. B. WATKIN
SUPT OF VAVAU CIRCUIT

REV. S. BAKER
PREMIER

PRINCE WELLINGTON
GOV. OF VAVAU

THE
ADVENTURES
UNLIMITED
CATALOG

Ancient Tonga

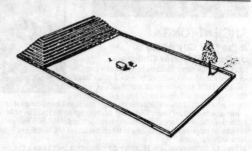

MYSTIC TRAVELLER SERIES

MYSTERY CITIES OF THE MAYA
Exploration and Adventure in Lubaantun & Belize
by Thomas Gann

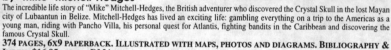

First published in 1925, Mystery Cities of the Maya is a classic in Central American archaeology-adventure. Gann was close friends with Mike Mitchell-Hedges, the British adventurer who discovered the famous crystal skull with his adopted daughter Sammy and Lady Richmond Brown, their benefactress. Gann battles pirates along Belize's coast and goes upriver with Mitchell-Hedges to the lost city of Lubaantun where they excavate a strange lost city where the crystal skull was discovered. Lubaantun is a unique city in the Mayan world as it is built out of precisely carved blocks of stone without the usual plaster-cement facing. Lubaantun contained several large pyramids partially destroyed by earthquakes and a large

amount of artifacts. Gann was a keen archaeologist, a member of the Mayan society, and shared Michell-Hedges belief in Atlantis and lost civilizations, pre-Mayan, in Central America and the Caribbean. Lots of good photos, maps and diagrams from the 20s.
252 PAGES, 6x9 PAPERBACK. ILLUSTRATED. $16.95. CODE: MCOM

DANGER MY ALLY
The Amazing Life Story of the Discoverer of the Crystal Skull
by "Mike" Michell-Hedges

The incredible life story of "Mike" Mitchell-Hedges, the British adventurer who discovered the Crystal Skull in the lost Mayan city of Lubaantun in Belize. Mitchell-Hedges has lived an exciting life: gambling everything on a trip to the Americas as a young man, riding with Pancho Villa, his personal quest for Atlantis, fighting bandits in the Caribbean and discovering the famous Crystal Skull.
374 PAGES, 6x9 PAPERBACK. ILLUSTRATED WITH MAPS, PHOTOS AND DIAGRAMS. BIBLIOGRAPHY & INDEX. $16.95. CODE: DMA

IN SECRET MONGOLIA
Sequel to Men & Gods In Mongolia
by Henning Haslund

Danish-Swedish explorer Haslund's first book on his exciting explorations in Mongolia and Central Asia. Haslund takes us via camel caravan to the medieval world of Mongolia, a country still barely known today. First published by Kegan Paul of London in 1934, this rare travel adventure back in print after 50 years. Haslund and his camel caravan journey across the Gobi Desert. He meets with renegade generals and warlords, god-kings and shamans. Haslund is captured, held for ransom, thrown into prison, battles black magic and portrays in vivid detail the birth of new nation. Haslund's second book *Men & Gods In Mongolia* is also available from Adventures Unlimited Press.
374 PAGES, 6x9 PAPERBACK. ILLUSTRATED WITH MAPS, PHOTOS AND DIAGRAMS. BIBLIOGRAPHY & INDEX. $16.95. CODE: ISM

MEN & GODS IN MONGOLIA
by Henning Haslund

First published in 1935 by Kegan Paul of London, Haslund takes us to the lost city of Karakota in the Gobi desert. We meet the Bodgo Gegen, a God-king in Mongolia similar to the Dalai Lama of Tibet. We meet Dambin Jansang, the dreaded warlord of the "Black Gobi." There is even material in this incredible book on the Hi-mori, an "airhorse" that flies through the air (similar to a Vimana) and carries with it the sacred stone of Chintamani. Aside from the esoteric and mystical material, there is plenty of just plain adventure: caravans across the Gobi desert, kidnapped and held for ransom, initiation into Shamanic societies, warlords, and the violent birth of a new nation.
358 PAGES, 6x9 PAPERBACK. 57 PHOTOS, ILLUSTRATIONS AND MAPS. $15.95. CODE: MGM

IN SECRET TIBET
by Theodore Illion.

Reprint of a rare 30's travel book. Illion was a German traveller who not only spoke fluent Tibetan, but travelled in disguise through forbidden Tibet when it was off-limits to all outsiders. His incredible adventures make this one of the most exciting travel books ever published. Includes illustrations of Tibetan monks levitating stones by acoustics.
210 PAGES. 6x9 PAPERBACK. ILLUSTRATED. $15.95. CODE: IST

DARKNESS OVER TIBET
by Theodore Illion.

In this second reprint of the rare 30's travel books by Illion, the German traveller continues his travels through Tibet and is given the directions to a strange underground city. As the original publisher's remarks said, this is a rare account of an underground city in Tibet by the only Westerner ever to enter it and escape alive!
210 PAGES. 6x9 PAPERBACK. ILLUSTRATED. $15.95. CODE: DOT

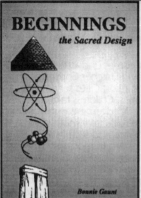

THE LOST CITIES

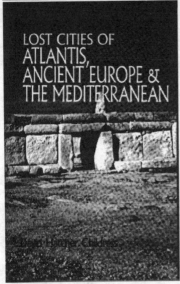

LOST CITIES OF
ATLANTIS,
ANCIENT EUROPE &
THE MEDITERRANEAN

LOST CITIES OF ATLANTIS, ANCIENT EUROPE & THE MEDITERRANEAN
David Hatcher Childress

Atlantis! The legendary lost continent comes under the close scrutiny of maverick archaeologist David Hatcher Childress. This sixth book in the internationally popular Lost Cities series takes us on quest for the lost continent of Atlantis. Childress takes the reader in search of sunken cities in the Mediterranean; across the Atlas Mountains in search of Atlantean ruins; to remote islands in search of megalithic ruins; living legengds and secret societies. From Ireland to Turkey, Morocco to Eastern Europe, or remote islands of the Mediterranean and Atlantic Childress takes the reader on an astonishing quest for mankind's past. Ancient technology, cataclysms, megalithic construction, lost civilizations and devastating wars of the past are all explored in this astonishing book. Childress challenges the skeptics and proves that great civilizations not only existed in the past, but the modern world and its problems are reflections of the ancient world of Atlantis.

524 pages, 6x9 paperback. Illustrated with 100s of maps, photos and diagrams. Bibliography & Index. $16.95. code: MED

LOST CITIES OF ANCIENT LEMURIA & THE PACIFIC
David Hatcher Childress

Was there once a continent in the Pacific? Called Lemuria or Pacifica by geologists, and Mu or Pan by the mystics, there is now ample mythological, geological and archaeological evidence to "prove" that an advanced, and ancient civilization once lived in the central Pacific. Maverick archaeologist and explorer David Hatcher Childress combs the Indian Ocean, Australia and the Pacific in search of the astonishing truth about mankind's past. Contains photos of the underwater city on Pohnpei, explanations on how the statues were levitated around Easter Island in a clock-wise vortex movement; disappearing islands; Egyptians in Australia; and more.

379 pages, 6x9, paperback. Photos, maps, and illustrations with Footnotes & Bibliography $14.95. code LEM

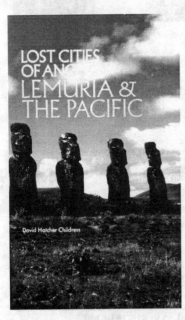

LOST CITIES
OF AN
LEMURIA &
THE PACIFIC

David Hatcher Childress

DAVID HATCHER CHILDRESS RADIO INTERVIEW

On the Lost Cities of North & Central America

In December of 1992, popular Lost Cities Series author, David Hatcher Childress, was interviewed live for six hours on the Laura Lee Radio Show, broadcast out of Seattle, Washington. The subject of the interview was David's book, Lost Cities of North and Central America, with special emphasis on the Smithsonian Institution's cover-up of American history. Other topics that were included in the interview, which also included live call-in questions, were pyramids around the world, the Rama Empire of India and Vimanas, Atlantis and Lemuria, UFOs, an Egyptian City in the Grand Canyon, and more! This audio interview comes on three high-quality 90 minute cassette tapes in boxes.

270 Minutes on 3 audio cassettes, $12.95 code: DHCR

THE LOST CITIES SERIES

LOST CITIES OF NORTH & CENTRAL AMERICA
David Hatcher Childress

From the jungles of Central America to the deserts of the southwest... down the back roads from coast to coast, maverick archaeologist and adventurer David Hatcher Childress takes the reader deep into unknown America. In this incredible book: search for lost Mayan cities and books of gold; discover an ancient canal system in Arizona; climb gigantic pyramids in the Midwest; explore megalithic monuments in New England; and join the astonishing quest for the lost cities throughout North America. From the war-torn jungles of Guatemala, Nicaragua and Honduras to the deserts, mountains and fields of Mexico, Canada, and the U.S.A., Childress takes the reader in search of sunken ruins; Viking forts; strange tunnel systems,; living dinosaurs; early Chinese explorers; and fantastic gold treasure. Packed with both early and current maps, photos and illustrations. An incredible life on the road in search of the ancient mysteries of the past!
590 pages, 6 x9, paperback. Photos, maps, and illustrations with Footnotes & Bibliography $14.95. code NCA

LOST CITIES & ANCIENT MYSTERIES OF AFRICA & ARABIA
David Hatcher Childress

Across ancient deserts, dusty plains and steaming jungles, maverick archaeologist David Childress continues his world-wide quest for lost cities and ancient mysteries. Join him as he discovers forbidden cities in the Empty Quarter of Arabia, "Atlantean" ruins in Egypt and the Kalahari desert; a mysterious, ancient empire in the Sahara; and more. This is an extraordinary life on the road: across war-torn countries Childress searches for King Solomon's Mines, living dinosaurs, the Ark of the Covenant and the solutions to the fantastic mysteries of the past.
423 pages, 6 x9, paperback. Photos, maps, and illustrations with Footnotes & Bibliography $14.95. code AFA

LOST CITIES & ANCIENT MYSTERIES OF SOUTH AMERICA
David Hatcher Childress

Rogue adventurer and maverick archaeologist, David Hatcher Childress, takes the reader on unforget-table journeys deep into deadly jungles, windswept mountains and scorching deserts in search of lost civilizations and ancient mysteries. Travel with David and explore stone cities high in mountain forests and fantastic tales of Inca treasure, living dinosaurs, and a mysterious tunnel system. Whether he is hopping freight trains, searching for secret cities, or just dealing with the daily problems, of food, money, and romance, the author keeps the reader spellbound. Includes both early and current maps, photos, and illustrations, and plenty of advice for the explorer planning his or her own journey of discovery.
381 pages, 6x9, paperback. Photos, maps, and illustrations with Footnotes & Bibliography $14.95. code SAM

LOST CITIES OF CHINA, CENTRAL INDIA & ASIA
David Hatcher Childress

Like a real life "Indiana Jones," maverick archaeologist David Childress takes the reader on an incredible adventure across some of the world's oldest and most remte countries in search of lost cities and ancient mysteries. Discover ancient cities in the Gobi Desert; hear fantastic tales of lost continents, vanished civilizations and secret societies bent on ruling the world. Visit forgotten monasteries in forbidding snow-capped mountains with strange tunnels to mysteri-ous subterranean cities! A unique combination of far-out exploration and practical travel advice; it will astound and delight the experienced traveler or the armchair voyager.
429 pages, 6 x9, paperback. Photos, maps, and illustrations with Footnotes & Bibliography $14.95. code CHI

Please use item codes when ordering http://www.azstarnet.com/~aup

ANTI-GRAVITY

UNDERGROUND BASES & TUNNELS
What is the Government Trying to Hide?
by Richard Sauder Ph.D.

Working from government documents and corporate records, Sauder has compiled an impressive book that digs below the surface of the military's super-secret underground! Go behind the scenes into little-known corners of the public record and discover how corporate America has worked hand-in-glove with the Pentagon for decades, dreaming about, planning-and actually constructing-secret underground bases. This book includes chapters on the locations of the bases, the tunneling technology, various military designs for underground bases, nuclear testing & underground bases, abductions, needles & implants; Is the U.S. Military Involved in "Alien" Cattle Mutilations?, more. 50 page photo & map insert.

201 PAGES, 6X9 PAPERBACK. WELL ILLUSTRATED. $15.95. CODE: UGB

MAN-MADE UFOS 1944—1994
Fifty Years of Suppression
Renato Vesco & David Hatcher Childress

A comprehensive and in-depth look at the early "flying saucer technology" of Nazi Germany and the genesis of early man-made UFOs from the captured German scientists, to escaped battalions of Germans to secret communities in South America and Antarctica to todays state-of-the-art "Dreamland" flying machines? Heavily illustrated, this astonishing book blows the lid off the "Government UFO Conspiracy" and explains with technical diagrams the technology involved. Examined in detail are secret underground airfields and factories; German secret weapons; "suction" aircraft; the origin of NASA; gyroscopic stabilizers and engines; the secret Marconi aircraft factory in South America; and more. Not to be missed by students of technology suppression, secret societies, anti-gravity, free energy conspiracy and World War II! Introduction by W.A. Harbinson, author of the Dell novels GENESIS and REVELATION.

318 PAGES, 6X9 TRADEPAPER. ILLUSTRATED. INDEX & FOOTNOTES. $16.95. CODE: MMU

THE FREE-ENERGY DEVICE HANDBOOK
A Compilation of Patents and Reports
David Hatcher Childress

A large format compilation of various patents, papers, descriptions and diagrams concerning free-energy devices and systems is a visual tool for experimenters and researchers into magnetic motors and other "over-unity" devices. With chapters on the Adams Motor, the Hans Coler Generator, cold fusion, superconductors, "N" machines, space-energy generators Nikola Tesla, T. Townsend Brown, and the latest in free-energy devices. Packed with photos, technical diagrams, patents and fascinating information, this book belongs on every science shelf. With energy and profit being a major political reason for fighting various wars, Free-Energy Devices, if ever allowed to be mass-distributed to consumers, could change the world! Get your copy now before the Department of Energy bans this book!

292 PAGES, 8X10 TRADEPAPER. PROFUSELY ILLUSTRATED. BIBLIOGRAPHY & APPENDIX. $16.95. CODE: FEH

EXTRATERRESTRIAL ARCHAEOLOGY
David Hatcher Childress

With 100s of photos and illustrations, Extra-Terrestrial Archaeology takes the reader to the strange and fascinating worlds of Mars, the Moon, Mercury, Venus, Saturn and other planets for a look at the alien structures that appear there. Using official NASA and Soviet photos, as well as other photos taken via telescope, this book seeks to prove that many of the planets (and moons) of our solar system are in some way inhabited by intelligent life. The book includes many blow-ups of NASA photos and detailed diagrams of structures-particularly on the Moon.

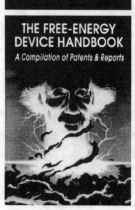

THE FREE-ENERGY DEVICE HANDBOOK
A Compilation of Patents & Reports

•NASA PHOTOS OF PYRAMIDS AND DOMED CITIES ON THE MOON.
•PYRAMIDS AND GIANT STATUES ON MARS.
•HOLLOW MOONS ON MARS AND OTHER PLANETS.
•ROBOT MINING VEHICLES THAT MOVE ABOUT THE MOON PROCESSING VALUABLE METALS.
•NASA & RUSSIAN PHOTOS OF SPACE-BASES ON MARS AND ITS MOONS.
•A BRITISH SCIENTIST WHO DISCOVERED A TUNNEL ON THE MOON, AND OTHER "BOTTOMLESS CRATERS"
•EARLY CLAIMS OF TRIPS TO THE MOON AND MARS.
•STRUCTURAL ANOMALIES ON VENUS, SATURN, JUPITER, MERCURY,URANUS & NEPTUNE.
•NASA, THE MOON AND ANTI-GRAVITY. PLUS MORE. HIGHLY ILLUSTRATED WITH PHOTOS, DIAGRAMS AND MAPS!
224 PAGES, 81/2 X11, PAPERBACK, BIBLIOGRAPHY, INDEX, APPENDIX. $18.95. CODE: ETA

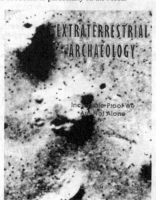

NATIVE AMERICAN STUDIES

THE HIAWATHA LEGENDS
North American Indian Lore
by Henry R. Schoolcraft

The Hiawatha Legends was first published in 1856. The myth of Hiawatha and other oral legends are derived from the story telling in the wigwams. A fascinating book of legends including chapters on such legends as Osseo, the Son of the Evening Star; The Star Family or the Celestial Sisters; the Red Swan; Legends of the Mastondon; the Magician of Lake Superior; Onaiazo, the Sky-Walker, A Legend of a Visit to the Sun; Bokwewa the Humpback Magician (Kokopeli?); Iosco or the Prairie Boy's Visit to the Sun and Moon; the Enchanted Moccasins; the Sun-Catcher; the Pictured Rocks of Lake Superior; legends of Red Haired People; more.

272 PAGES, 6x9 PAPERBACK. ILLUSTRATED. $12.95. CODE: THL

SIX MONTHS AMONG INDIANS, WOLVES & WILD ANIMALS
The Historical Account of the Winter of 1839/1840
by Darius Cook

Six Months Among Indians, Wolves & Wild Animals was written by a young newspaperman named Darius Cook. It tells of his adventures in 1839 as a Michigan pioneer who experienced winter's biting cold, the silences in the big woods, the full game, snarling wolves beyond the firelight... as well as the Indian tales told to him firsthand by Chiefs Noonday and Sagemaw about their last days of the old hunting grounds. Interesting tales of the death of Tecumseh, Saginaw, Indian legends and stories, and of Cook's various narrow escapes with bears, wolves, and War Parties. An exact reprint of the 1889 edition with great original illustrations of such chiefs as Saginaw, Adaniram Judson, Tecumseh and others.

108 PAGES, 6x9 PAPERBACK. ILLUSTRATED. $10.95. CODE: 6MI

THE DIFFUSION ISSUE
Edited by Donald Cyr

A large format book on the controversial issue of ancient seafarers and the theory of ancient contacts (diffusion) of culture, science and civilization around the world. This book includes articles on Pre-Columbian transoceanic contacts, Chinese ancient world mapageing, Megalithic man in America, and new world plants in the old world.

122 PAGES, 9x10 TRADEPAPER, ILLUSTRATED WITH PHOTOGRAPHS & DIAGRAMS. $9.95. CODE: TDI

THE ECCLECTIC EPIGRAPHER
Edited by Donald Cyr

Ogam writing around the world; m e g a l i t h s a n d a n c i e n t inscriptions, Professor Barry Fell on Epigraphy, more.

160 PAGES, 10 x12 TRADEPAPER, ILLUSTRATED WITH INDEX, REFERENCES & BIBLIOGRAPHY $9.95 CODE: ECE

EXPLORING ROCK ART
Edited by Donald Cyr with Barry Fell

A fascinating look at the bizarre and controversial rock art, including the Illinois Thunderbird monster called the Piasa (believed by many to have been a gigantic flying lizard!), Colorado Ogam inscriptions, megaliths, pyramids and rock art in Scandinavia and more are all profiled in this large format book.

128 PAGES, 8x10 TRADEPAPER, 100 PHOTOS, ILLUSTRATIONS AND MAPS. $9.95 CODE: ERA

NATIVE AMERICAN MYTHS & MYSTERIES
Vincent H. Gaddis

Veteran Fortean researcher Gaddis's classic book on strange Native American myths and legends. The tribal shamanic knowledge links Native Americans today to this spiritual past, many thousands of years old. Divination and healing ceremonies, the Shaking Tent mystery, Navaho feather magic and other traditions all portend a great knowledge lost to the European colonizers. This book, written by one of the finest researchers of our age, will astound, fascinate and enlighten you to an ancient world hidden in the American landscape.

184 PAGES, 6x9 PAPERBACK. $12.95. CODE: NAM

THE COLORADO OGAM ALBUM
Photographs of Ancient Inscriptions
Donald Cyr

A large format book from Stonehenge Viewpoint with page after page of ancient inscriptions found at some of the river terminus sites in Colorado. Plenty of interesting ogam writing and other rock inscriptions, plus interesting chapters on the Olmecs and Ogam; the Chinese connection; 23 chapters in all.

128 PAGES, 10x12 TRADEPAPER. ILLUSTRATED WITH PHOTOS, CHARTS & DRAWINGS. INDEX. $12.95. CODE: COA

Primitive Man in Michigan

Prehistoric Indian cliff painting

PRIMITIVE MAN IN MICHIGAN 24 HOUR CREDIT CARD ORDERS—CALL:
Indians and Michigan Prehistory
by W. B. Hinsdale

A reprint of a fascinating and well illustrated volume on the huge earthworks, mounds, tools, artifacts, rock carvings and more. Despite its title, this book shows us what a sophisticated civlization once occupied the Great Lakes region. Important chapters on the massive earthworks, ancient pyramids, garden plots, trepanned skulls, more.

229 PAGES, 6x9 PAPERBACK, ILLUSTRATED. $12.95 CODE:PRMM

NATIVE AMERICAN STUDIES

TZOLKIN
Visionary Perspectives and Calendar Studies
John Major Jenkins

TZOLKIN is a visionary journey into the heart of an ancient oracle. Jenkins, in both academic and mystical viewpoints, explore the sacred Calendar of Mezoamerica is than a calendar, but an ancient cosmology that includes a mytho-evolutionary system which describes the spiritual and physical unfolding of the Earth. At the heart of this sophisticated philosophy is the Sacred Tree—the Axis Mundi. Prepare for a journey... prepare to to enter the mysterious borderland between night and day!

346 PAGES. 6X9 TRADEPAPER. PROFUSELY ILLUSTRATED. $13.95. CODE: TZO

AMERICAN DISCOVERY
The Real Story
Gunnar Thompson.

Thompson's second book is a state-of-the-art overview of ancient voyages to America, beginning with the Native Americans and continuing through Amerigo Vespucci. The book features Old World art in America, ancient maps of America, chapters on native tribes; Phoenicians; Norse; Celts, Britons, Irish & Welsh; Greeks, Jews & Romans; Japanese; Hindus; Indonesians; Sumerians; Chinese; Black Africans; Scots, Basques, & Portuguese; Polynesians; Egyptians & Arabs. Archaeologist Thompson explores the reasons why Old World voyagers sailed to America and their impact on native culture. Diffusion of plants, diseases, languages, symbols, races, religion, metals, and civilization are examined.100s of illustrations and photos.

400 PAGES, 6X9 TRADEPAPER, PROFUSELY ILLUSTRATED, BIBLIOGRAPHY & INDEX. $17.95. CODE: AMD

ANCIENT EGYPTIAN SURVIVALS IN THE PACIFIC
by R.A. Jairazbhoy

Archaeologist and historian Jairazbhoy explores the evidence for ancient Egyptian voyages across the Indian Ocean and the Pacific in early prehistory. Jairazbhoy gives concludes that the Egyptians voyaged across the Pacific to North and South America and this book examines "the Egyptian imprint" that has been retained on many Pacific islands, including Easter Island. Other chapters on the Egyptian sources of Polynesian belief, Easter Island as a secret Egyptian trading base between Egypt and Peru, more.

98 PAGES, 6X9 PAPERBACK. ILLUSTRATED. FOOTNOTES & BIBLIOGRAPHY. $11.95. CODE: AESP

RAMESES III
Father of Ancient America
by R.A. Jairazbhoy

Archaeologist and historian Jairazbhoy brings us this fascinating and scholarly look at the evidence for ancient Egyptian voyages to the Americas in early prehistory. Packed with photographic and other evidence, Jairazbhoy reconstructs Rameses III's wish to find an earthly paradise. This adventure led him to the Americas, where the ancient Egyptians mingled with the native meso-American cultures.

148 PAGES, 6X9 PAPERBACK. ILLUSTRATED. FOOTNOTES & BIBLIOGRAPHY. $11.95. CODE: RAM3

ANIMATED EARTH
Metaphysics & the Whistling Pots of Peru
by Daniel K. Statnekov

An unusual adventure story in wich Statnekov is sent on a shamanic quest to Peru to discover the cosmic secret to the whistling vessels that are to be found there. An archaeological adventure of the spirit that illuminates a unusual subject. Something of interest here perhaps for students of harmonics, sound and vibration.

227 PAGES, 6X9 PAPERBACK. 8 PAGE COLOR INSERT. OTHER ILLUSTRATIONS & PHOTOS. INDEX. $9.95. CODE: ANE

THE LOST PYRAMIDS OF ROCK LAKE
Frank Joseph

40 miles west of Milwaukee lies the pyramid complex of Aztalan and the sunken ruins of Rock Lake. For years rumors of a lost city in the lake have circulated and finally in 1989 a side-scan sonar mapping of the lake was done. This book recounts that expedition and gives the reader background information on the mysteries of Wisconsin. See also ATLANTIS IN WISCONSIN.

212 PAGES, 6X9 PAPERBACK. ILLUSTRATED. FOOTNOTES & BIBLIOGRAPHY. $10.95. CODE: TLP

THE MYSTERY CAVE OF MANY FACES
A History of Burrow's Cave
Russell Burrows & Fred Ridholm.

This hardback book tells the incredible story of how Russell Burrows discovered a cave of thousands of fantastic artifacts in April of 1982. The cave's walled up entrance in a remote valley of southern Illinois kept one of the most astonishing archaeological discoveries hidden for approximately 2000 years. This discovery, and photos of the artifacts, have created a sensation in the archaeology field, and some well-known scholars, such as Barry Fell, have declared much of the collection to be a fake. Others, such as Joseph Mahan, maintain that the thousands of ancient Hindu, Egyptian, Sumerian and other artifacts, are genuine, and that the cave is but one of a number of such caches. This book chronicles the exciting discovery of the cave, the trials and dangers of getting the story to the public, and a brief description of some of the many artifacts found inside, including statues, coins, engraved tablets, various texts and more. Well illustrated with photos and drawings of the artifacts from the cave.

254 PAGES, 6X9 HARDBACK, PROFUSELY ILLUSTRATED, BIBLIOGRAPHY & INDEX. $24.95. CODE: TMC

PHILOSOPHY & RELIGION

THE CHRISTIAN CONSPIRACY
How the Teachings of Christ Have Been Altered by Christians
Dr. David L. Moore
Is is Christianity or is it Heresy? In the first five centuries after the Crucifixion, a series of politically sponsored ecumenical councils were held to determine church doctrine. The winners at these meetings defined the nature of Christianity, the contents of the Bible, and acceptable interpretations of the gospel. The loser were labeled heretics. Dr. Moore looks into the circumstances and doctrine changes, including chapters on the Cathars, reincarnation and early Christian beliefs, the nature of Christ, lost books of the Bible, the history of the first five councils, more.
347 PAGES, 6x9 TRADEPAPER. ILLUSTRATED. $14.95. CODE: CHC

A PERSONAL PATHWAY TO GOD
Our Song of Freedom
Dr. L. David Moore
Christian Conspiracy author Dr. L. David Moore answers the question of what the major religions all have in common, though their messages have been distorted. Moore traces the unified messages of God in all of the world's major religions, and consolidates them into four COSMIC TRUTHS. He then illustrates the nature of spiritual growth with stories of his own personal past.
288 PAGES, 6x9 PAPERBACK. BIBLIOGRAPHY & INDEX. $13.95. CODE: PPG

CHRISTIANITY AND THE NEW AGE RELIGION
A Bridge Toward Mutual Understanding
Dr. L. David Moore
Many of the "New Age" deny the rich heritage and understanding developed by Christianity, while many of the Christian heritage deny the understanding of the New Age. This book is attempt to bridge understanding between the two, and makes an effort to take a religious philosophy that spans our planet into a religion that spans the Universe. 9 chapters in all.
244 PAGES, 6x9 TRADEPAPER. $12.95. CODE: CNA

THE KAHUNA RELIGION OF HAWAII
David Kaonohiokala Bray & Douglas Low
From generation to generation since ancient times, the Hawaiians passed down the secret knowledge of spiritual power and sacred knowledge. This is a personal account of Kahuna by the well known native Hawaiian priest 'Daddy Bray' and Douglas Low, a college professor who was in training with Bray for 12 years. Includes detailed instructions on the unique spiritual pathway through ancient Polynesian worlds of creation.
66 PAGES. 6x9 TRADEPAPER. ILLUSTRATED. $8.95. CODE: KRH

THE UNVARNISHED NEW TESTAMENT
A New Translation From the Original Greek
Translated by Andy Gaus.
This new, innovative translation on of the New Testament opens the closed doors of perconception and allows the reader to veiw these important Greek writings in an entirely different light. Most translations of the New Testament are made by committees; they interpret the original text through theological doctrines and dogmas which arose centuries after the books were written. In this translation, Andy Gaus presents the New Testament as it would have apageseared to someone reading the oringinal, unvarnished Greek—as though 2,000 years of Christian history had not occurred. Gone are the double columns, small type, and verse numbers common to other editions By eliminating these obstacles, the reader can encounter the stunning directness of the words themselves.
508 PAGES, 6x9 TRADEPAPER. $16.95. CODE: UNT

THE AQUARIAN GOSPEL OF JESUS THE CHRIST
Transcribed From the Akashic Records
by Levi
This popular book, first published at the turn of the century, is the amazing story of Jesus, the man from Galilee, and how he attained the Christ consciousness open to all men. It includes a compete record of the "lost" 18 years of his life, a time which the New Testament is strangely silent. During this period Jesus travelled widely in India, Tibet, Persia, Egypt and Greece, learning from the Masters, seers and wisemen of the East and the West in their temples and schools. Included in this amazing book is information on the Council of the Seven Sages of the World, Jesus with the Chinese Master Mencius (Meng Tzu) in Tibet, the ministry, trial, execution and resurrection of Jesus.
270 PAGES, 6x9 PAPERBACK. $14.95. CODE: AGJC

24 HOUR CREDIT CARD ORDERS—CALL: 815-253-6390 FAX: 815-253-6300
EMAIL: AUP@AZSTARNET.COM   HTTP://WWW.AZSTARNET.COM/~AUP

ANTI-GRAVITY

THE ANTI-GRAVITY HANDBOOK

Edited by David Hatcher Childress, With Arthur C. Clarke, Nikola Tesla, T.B. Paulicki, Bruce Cathie, Leonard G. Cramp and Albert Einstein

The new expanded compilation of material on Anti-Gravity, Free Energy, Flying Saucer propulsion, UFOs, Suppressed Technology, NASA Cover-ups and more. Highly illustrated with patents, technical illustrationsand photos. This revised and expanded edition has more material, including photos of Area 51, Nevada, the government's secret testing facility. This classic on weird science is back in a 90s format!
- **How to build a flying saucer.**
- **Read about Arthur C. Clarke on Anti-Gravity.**
- **learn about crystals and their role in levitation.**
- **Secret government research and developement.**
- **Nikola Tesla on how anti-gravity airships could draw power from the atmosphere.**
- **Bruce Cathie's Anti-Gravity Equation.**
- **NASA, the Moon and Anti-Gravity. Plus more.**

230 PAGES, 7x10 TRADEPAPER, BIBLIOGRAPHY/INDEX/APPENDIX. HIGHLY ILLUSTRATED WITH 100'S OF PATENTS ILLUSTRATIONS AND PHOTOS, $14.95. CODE: AGH

ANTI-GRAVITY & THE WORLD GRID

Edited by David Hatcher Childress

Is the earth surrounded by an intricate electromagnetic grid network offering free energy? This compilation of material on the earth grid, ley lines, and world power points contains chapters on the geography, mathematics, and light harmonics of the earth grid. Learn the purpose of ley lines and ancient megalithic structures located on the grid. Discover how the grid made the Philadelphia Experiment possible. Explore the Coral Castle and many other mysteries; Including, acoustic levitation, Tesla Shields and Scalar Wave weaponry. Browse through the section on anti-gravity patents, and research resources.

274 PAGES, 150 RARE PHOTOGRAPHS, DIAGRAMS AND DRAWINGS, 7x10 PAPERBACK, $14.95. CODE: AGW

ANTI-GRAVITY
& THE UNIFIED FIELD

Edited by David Hatcher Childress

Is Einstein's Unified Field theory the answer to all of our energy problems? Explored in this compilation of material is how gravity, electricity and magnetism manifest from a unified field around us. Why artificial gravity is possible; Secrets of UFO propulsion; free energy; Nikola Tesla and anti-gravity airships of the 20's and 30's; Flying saucers as superconducting whirls of plasma; anti-mass generators; vortex propulsion; suppressed technology; government cover-ups; gravitational pulse drive, spacecraft & more.

240 PAGES, 7x10 PAPERBACK,130 RARE PHOTOGRAPHS, DIAGRAMS AND DRAWINGS, $14.95. CODE: AGU

ETHER TECHNOLOGY

A Rational Approach to Gravity Control
Rho Sigma

This classic book on Anti-Gravity & Free Energy is back in print and back in stock. Written by a well-known American scientist under the pseudonym of "Rho Sigma," this book delves into International efforts at gravity control and discoid craft propulsion. Before the Quantum Field, there was "Ether." This small, but informative books has chapters on John Searle and "Searle discs;" T. Townsend Brown and his work on Anti-Gravity; Ether-Vortex-Turbines: Includes a forward by former NASA astronaut Edgar Mitchell. Don't miss this classic book!

108 PAGES, 6x9 TRADEPAPER, ILLUSTRATED WITH PHOTOS & DIAGRAMS. $12.95. CODE: ETT

24 HOUR CREDIT CARD ORDERS—CALL: 815-253-6390 FAX: 815-253-6300
EMAIL: AUP@AZSTARNET.COM HTTP://WWW.AZSTARNET.COM/~AUP

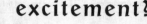

One Adventure Place
P.O. Box 74
Kempton, Illinois 60946
United States of America
Tel.: 815-253-6390 • Fax: 815-253-6300
Email: aup@azstarnet.com
http://www.azstarnet.com/~aup

ORDERING INSTRUCTIONS

➤ Remit by USD$ Check or Money Order
➤ Credit Cards: Visa, MasterCard, Discovery, &
American Express Accepted
➤ Call ♦ Fax ♦ Email Any Time

SHIPPING CHARGES

United States

➤ Postal Book Rate { $2.00 First Item / 50¢ Each Additional Item
➤ Priority Mail { $3.50 First Item / $1.50 Each Additional Item
➤ UPS { $3.50 First Item / $1.00 Each Additional Item
NOTE: UPS Delivery Available to Mainland USA Only

Canada

➤ Postal Book Rate { $3.00 First Item / $1.00 Each Additional Item
➤ Postal Air Mail { $4.00 First Item / $2.00 Each Additional Item
➤ Personal Checks or Bank Drafts MUST BE
USD$ and Drawn on a US Bank
➤ Canadian Postal Money Orders OK
➤ Payment MUST BE USD$

All Other Countries

➤ Surface Delivery { $5.00 First Item / $2.00 Each Additional Item
➤ Postal Air Mail { $10.00 First Item / $8.00 Each Additional Item
➤ Payment MUST BE USD$
➤ Checks MUST BE USD$ and
Drawn on a US Bank
➤ Add $5.00 for Air Mail Subscription to
Future *Adventures Unlimited* Catalogs

SPECIAL NOTES

➤ RETAILERS: Standard Discounts Available
➤ BACKORDERS: We Backorder all Out-of-
Stock Items Unless Otherwise Requested
➤ PRO FORMA INVOICES: Available on Request
➤ VIDEOS: NTSC Mode Only
PAL & SECAM Mode Videos Are Not Available

European Office:
Adventures Unlimited, PO Box 372,
Dronten, 8250 AJ, The Netherlands
South Pacific Office
Adventures Unlimited NZ
221 Symonds Sreet Box 8199
Auckland, New Zealnd

Please check: ☑

☐ This is my first order	☐ I have ordered before	☐ This is a new address

Name	
Address	
City	

State/Province	Postal Code

Country	

Phone day	Evening

Fax	

Item Code	Item Description	Price	Qty	Total

Please check: ☑

☐ Postal-Surface	Subtotal ➤
	Less Discount-10% for 3 or more items ➤
☐ Postal-Air Mail (Priority in USA)	Balance ➤
	Illinois Residents 7% Sales Tax ➤
	Previous Credit ➤
☐ UPS (Mainland USA only)	Shipping ➤
	Total (check/MO in USD$ only) ➤

☐ Visa/MasterCard/Discover/Amex

Card Number	
Expiration Date	

10% Discount When You Order 3 or More Items!

Comments & Suggestions	Share Our Catalog with a Friend